Alleluias of the Mind

Other Books of Interest from St. Augustine's Press

Zbigniew Janowski, *Homo Americanus:*
The Rise of Totalitarian Democracy in America

Predrag Cicovacki, *The Ethic of the Upward Gaze:*
Essays Inspired by Immanuel Kant and Nicolai Hartmann

Leo Strauss, *Leo Strauss' Published but Uncollected English Writings*

Michael Davis, *Electras: Aeschylus, Sophocles, and Euripides*

D. Q. McInerny, *Being Philosophical*

Gabriel Marcel, *Toward Another Kingdom: Two Dramas of the Darker Years*

Gabriel Marcel, *The Invisible Threshold: Two Plays by Gabriel Marcel*

D. C. Schindler, *God and the City*

Gene Fendt, *Camus' Plague: Myth for Our World*

Roger Scruton, *The Politics of Culture and Other Essays*

Nalin Ranasinghe, *Shakespeare's Reformation:*
Christian Humanism and the Death of God

Francisco Insa, *The Formation of Affectivity: A Christian Approach*

Daniel J. Mahoney, *Recovering Politics, Civilization, and the Soul:*
Essays on Pierre Manent and Roger Scruton

Pierre Manent, *The Religion of Humanity: The Illusion of Our Times*

Stanley Rosen, *The Language of Love: An Interpretation of Plato's Phaedrus*

James M. Rhodes, *Knowledge, Sophistry, and Scientific Politics:*
Plato's Dialogues Theaetetus, Sophist, and Statesman

Michael Franz (editor), *Eric Voegelin's Late Meditations and Essays:*
Critical Commentary Companions

John von Heyking, *Comprehensive Judgment and Absolute Selflessness:*
Winston Churchill on Politics as Friendship

Winston Churchill, *Savrola*

Winston Churchill, *The River War*

Winston Churchill, *My Early Life*

Alleluias of the Mind

The Songs of Aquinas

DAKIN MATTHEWS

ST. AUGUSTINE'S PRESS

South Bend, Indiana

Manufactured in the United States of America.

1 2 3 4 5 6 29 28 27 26 25 24

Library of Congress Control Number: 2024940220

Paperback ISBN: 978-1-58731-014-0
ebook ISBN: 978-1-58731-019-5

∞ The paper used in this publication meets the minimum
requirements of the American National Standard for Information Sciences –
Permanence of Paper for Printed Materials, ANSI Z39.48-1984.

St. Augustine's Press
www.staugustine.net

For Father John Olivier P.S.S.,
who taught me hymns from the age of twelve,
and introduced me to Broadway musicals
at the age of fourteen,
but sadly did not live long enough to see me
perform in one sixty years later.

TABLE OF CONTENTS

INTRODUCTION

Alleluias of the Mind

I start with the title—because in a sense, the title says it all.

This is first of all an attempt to translate—in all its richness—a phrase from one of the songs themselves—the greatest of the songs in my opinion, the *Lauda Sion*. The phrase is *"mentis jubilatio"*—literally, "jubilation of the mind"—from the fifth verse, here in the Latin and in Joseph Connelly's prose translation (p. 124):

Sit laus plena, sit sonora,	Therefore let our praise be full and
Sit jucunda, sit decora	resounding and our soul's rejoicing
Mentis jubilatio.	full of delight and beauty.

So much more is loaded into that verse, and that phrase, than the translation reveals. First of all, there sits behind it the technical theology of hymns, a subject Aquinas actually wrote an article about in the *Summa* (2-2.91.2). There, he asks and answers (as is his practice) the question: whether it's all right for people to sing when they praise God.

In the *Summa,* this question arises as Aquinas works his way through the virtues and vices. Under the topic of "justice" he places "religion"; under "religion" he explores the ten commandments; and under the first three commandments, he explores topics like worshiping, swearing by, praying to, and praising God.

When he gets to the question of praising God in song, he rejects arguments against the practice, and notes (rather drily) that if human beings need to make their praises out loud (and, he maintains, they *do*—not so much so that God can hear them, but so that the listeners and the speakers themselves can be drawn up by them to God), all the more reason that they should *sing* them out loud, since different human souls respond differently to different melodies, and the weaker ones, which are so susceptible to being moved by music, can thereby be more easily moved to proper devotion. It's probably not as aesthetic an answer as we might like, surely more utilitarian and even patronizing than we might prefer, but it is his answer nonetheless.

Now look at the adjectives, what they mean and how they operate. Something should be "*plena*" (full) and "*sonora*" (pleasing to the ear and resounding) and "*jucunda*" (delightful, pleasing) and "*decora*" (lovely but also proper)—but what is that "something"? Or is it more than one something? The syntax is not entirely clear.

The basic structure of these three lines seems to be a rhetorical figure called "chiasmus"—one of Shakespeare's favorites by the way—which simply means that there is a tweaking of the word order so that in structure the second half is a reverse image of the first. The first half of the stanza is noun-adjective-adjective (*laus, plena, sonora*), while the second half is adjective-adjective-noun (*jucunda, decora, jubilatio*). It would seem that the first two adjectives are predicated of "*laus*" (praise), while the second two are predicated of "*jubilatio*" (jubilation). In his translation, this is how Connelly reads it: let the praise be full and resounding, and the rejoicing, delightful and lovely.

There is much to suggest that Connelly is right in his distribution; the *prosodic* structure seems to favor an endline stop after the first line, and a run-on after the second, thus suggesting exactly the distribution he supposes. But I'm not sure the Latin verse absolutely requires it; all the adjectives are feminine in gender, so they might well be properties of both. In addition, the "*mentis jubilatio*" may itself be another predicate rather than a subject, so that it too identifies what the praise should be—"a rejoicing of the mind or soul." In that reading, the structure is more climactic that chiasmic, and the three lines build to the final phrase. There is just enough ambiguity to make both readings possible, and thus the verse becomes richer, more provocative, and perhaps more "poetic." *(I apologize for getting so technical, but that's part of what explication requires.)*

Next, the adjectives themselves are richer and more provocative than one might notice at first glance. For the praise part, "*sonora*" may mean "pleasing to the ear," but it may also mean simply "loud," while at the same time perhaps catching the "echoing" quality of religious singing, either because of the architecture of the church or the antiphonal style. That it should be coupled with *"plena"* ("full") lends further confirmation to the idea that singing is a kind of overflow, that the movement from speech to song involves an awareness of the need to unburden a full heart.

For the "jubilation" part, we should recall that for Aquinas, proportion and beauty were nearly synonymous, and *"decora"* catches both senses. And the *"jucunda"* adds the idea of not just "pleasing" to hear, but "pleasurable" to do; the music is not just pleasing to God, and pleasing to those who hear, but the act of praising in song is, in some sense, emotionally satisfying, perhaps even healthy, for the singer. Aquinas did know of such things; he wrote an article later in the same volume (*ST* 2-2.168.2) about how jokes and games are good for the soul no less than for the body; that the soul needs its relief as well and finds it in wit and playfulness, even at times in nonsense. And add to all that the fact that there is a kind of felicitous oxymoron in coupling *"jubilatio"* and *"decora,"* in that the first suggests almost an overflow, a "too-muchness" while the second suggests a loveliness of proportion and decorum.

So now we come to the phrase itself, *mentis jubilatio*—"the rejoicing of the mind or soul." *"Mens"*—literally "mind"—was a common substitute for *"anima"* ("soul"), especially in lyrics when a shorter word was needed— as in *"mens impletur gratia,"* for example, ("the soul is filled with grace") from Aquinas's vespers antiphon for Corpus Christi. As we have already seen, the act of praising and the praise itself become, in a sense, one thing in sung prayer, simultaneously a *"laus"* and a *"jubilatio."* But—and here is the Thomistic kicker—he may specifically be suggesting it is literally a *jubilatio* of the *mind*, of the *intellect*. Whatever he may have said in the *Summa* about religious music being good for the weaker human soul, here in the *Lauda Sion* I would like to think that he may be countering with the suggestion that the "mind" may occasionally break into song for the sheer pleasure of it.

If so, he ever so gently corrects Augustine, who praised the *jubilatio* of religious singing *without* words. As Willi Apel translates and interprets:

> St. Augustine (as well as other church fathers) repeatedly expressed the idea that the highest rejoicing of the soul calls for music without words: "If somebody is full of joyful exultation, . . . he bursts out in an exulting song without words"; or: "For

whom is this jubilation more proper than for the nameless God?
. . . And since you cannot name him and yet may not remain
silent, what else can you do but break out in jubilation so that
your heart may rejoice without words, and that the immensity
of your joy may not know the bounds of syllables." (Apel, p.
267)

Of course, Augustine was very likely speaking of the typical Ambrosian
chants he knew with their long syllabic cadences. But one senses in him as
well a discomfort with the idea of singing *about* God in any extended man-
ner—too much danger in the typical excesses of that kind of lyricism, too
many metaphorical traps laid for the imprecise theologian who lets himself
wander about in verbal melodies.

But not for Aquinas. Let your praise and your rejoicing be full, be loud,
be delightful, be lovely; let your mind—not just your heart, your *mind*—
make music—meaningful music. And how else can it do that but in lyrical
language? Again in Apel's translation and commentary:

In a Gradual, Alleluia, or Offertory word and song join hands
in the rendition of the liturgical prayer, the one contributing
the thought, the other what Thomas Aquinas called the "*exul-
tatio mentis, de aeternis habita, prorumpens in vocem*"—the ex-
ultation of the mind, derived from things eternal, bursting forth
in sound. (Apel, p. 267)

And finally, there is the possible self-referential liturgical pun on *jubi-
latio*. For a *jubilatio* was not just the experience of rejoicing, it echoes one
of the technical names of the musical (and sometimes verbal) extension of
the Alleluia chant that effectively became the Sequence, of which the *Lauda
Sion* is perhaps the finest late medieval example. The word "*Alleluia*" and
the word "*jubilus*" were associated from the earliest days of liturgical theory.
So a "*jubilus*" is an extension of an Alleluia, and—by extension—*is* an Al-
leluia; thus a "*jubilatio*" of the mind is not just the joyous mind at play, it
may also suggest an Alleluia extension with words (for without words, as
Thomas explains elsewhere, we cannot know our own hearts and minds).
I will speak more of this a little later in this preface, so let this summary

suffice here—except to add one final observation. If a *jubilatio mentis* is both a liturgical song and a mind filled to overflowing with joy, just think what you get when the mind in question is the mind of Aquinas. What you get is the *Lauda Sion*—an amazing Alleluia of a quite spectacular mind.

The Authorship Question

Unfortunately, we must confront now the thorny question of authorship. Did St. Thomas Aquinas actually write the *Lauda Sion* and the three hymns on which his reputation as a Latin poet exists? Though the traditional opinion is yes, the scholarly opinion is more hedged. I tend to think—based on tradition and internal evidence—that what we have in the songs themselves is substantially what came from his pen (or his dictation), but it would be dishonest not to report—however briefly—on the controversy.

The songs in question are three hymns and a sequence which are part of the Office and Mass for the Roman Catholic Feast of Corpus Christi. (The collection of lessons, hymns, responsories, antiphons, prayers, and bible readings proper to any feast is known as its "Office.") There is little doubt that Aquinas did compose an office for the feast; his contemporary biographer reported that Urban IV commissioned not one but two new offices for Corpus Christi from Aquinas in 1263 or 1264, in preparation for extending this Eucharistic feast to the Universal Church. But we also know that local Eucharistic festivals, particularly in Belgium, had their own offices, which antedated the pope's commission to Aquinas; and that there was a Roman office for the feast in existence by the end of the thirteenth century which could not have been Aquinas's. So the question is: is the current office—or at least, are the four songs in question—the work of Thomas Aquinas?

In all likelihood, the entire Office, as we now have it, cannot honestly be considered Thomas's exclusive and undoubted work. The texts of the present Office—and therefore of the four songs I am dealing with—were not attributed to him until the end of the fifteenth century, more than two hundred years after their supposed composition. We also know that the present Office shows very strong signs of being a compilation of offices—particularly from the Cistercian Office used at Liège in Belgium. We also know that the four songs show a marked dependence upon earlier hymns composed before 1264. All this leads one scholar to conclude that "we can definitely say that he [Aquinas] was not the author of the Office in its present form" (*CE,* "Corpus Christi").

Even granting the truth of all this, there is no evidence that he was *not* the author of these four songs. Liturgies were rarely circulated with an author's name attached. The songs have not been found to exist before 1264. No other author has ever been credited with their composition, and Church tradition almost from the very beginning has favored Aquinas. We know he composed at least one office for the feast, and that very likely meant writing new hymns—admittedly based on pre-existing models and sung to pre-existing melodies. And the four songs we have are, even the most carping critic will admit, "theologically and artistically worthy of the pen of Aquinas."

For me, the strongest evidence is the last. Especially in the *Lauda Sion,* the relationship between the theology of the sequence and Aquinas's other writings on the Eucharist makes a very persuasive case. The sequence is unmistakably "Thomistic"; why should it not be from his own hand? I am drawn almost inescapably to believe that here tradition has not erred. But in the end, it matters little. It is the songs themselves that matter, not the attribution; and we may continue speaking of Aquinas the lyricist, as we do of Homer the epic poet—though I think with far greater confidence.

His Life and Works

Josef Pieper and G. K. Chesterton have written the most useful introductions to the life and work of Thomas Aquinas available in English for the non-specialist. I urge any reader who wishes to pursue an association with Aquinas further to refer to either or both of these two wonderful little books. But for those who need an immediate refresher, here are the basic facts.

Thomasso D'Aquino was born in the castle-town of Roccasecca just outside Aquino in 1225. Though Italian by birth, he was of Germanic blood, certainly on his mother's side and possibly on his father's as well. His father was a minor noble and sent his youngest son to study at the Abbey School of Monte Cassino at the age of five; his education there, under the Benedictines, lasted until he was fifteen, when he fled from the monastic life to Naples and four years later joined—to his family's great disapproval—the Dominicans, one of the new mendicant or "begging" orders.

His Dominican brothers tried to smuggle him out of Naples and beyond the reach of his family, but his blood brothers kidnapped him on his way to Paris and locked him up in one of their father's castles. He was a prisoner for perhaps a year, before his family relented and let him continue on his journey to Paris. Once there, he enrolled in the University and became an undergraduate student of Albertus Magnus (Albert the Great) in 1245. He later followed his master to Cologne, continuing his studies (especially of neo-Platonism) there.

At the age of 27, his order recalled him to Paris, hoping to set him up there as a teacher, but university politics got in the way. The faculty, resenting the growing influence of the orders, organized a boycott against his classes, and it took a mandate from the pope to lift it. He held his teaching chair at Paris for only three years—three turbulent and influential years—and then set off on a lifetime of wandering and only temporary posts. He organized courses of study for the Dominicans in Italy, served as an adviser to Pope Urban IV in his court at Orvieto, then organized an academy for his order in Rome, then was summoned to serve the new Pope Clement IV at his court in Viterbo, and then was commanded by his order to return to the University of Paris, where the theological wars had turned very nasty indeed.

Those three years in Paris were the most productive—and bitterly controversial—of his life; and then abruptly in 1272, his superiors ordered him once again to Naples, to set up another college. A year and a half later in the midst of that, the pope ordered him to Lyons to participate in the General Council; on the way there, he fell ill and died. He was not yet fifty.

We may assume that his productive writing years extended from his return to Paris from Cologne (1252) to his death (1273), twenty-one years in all. He wrote constantly—at times, according to tradition, dictating three or four different works simultaneously to three of four different stenographers. At his death he had composed about a hundred items—some of quite astonishing length.

His great works are three: his Commentaries on Peter Lombard's *Sententiae*—essentially something like a Master's thesis required of all professional theologians; the *Summa Contra Gentiles,* a massive synthesis defending the faith against non-Christian philosophers; and the *Summa Theologiae,* another massive synthesis of the Catholic faith, this time written specifically for theology students. His commentaries (called the *Scripta*) were most likely written towards the end of his graduate studies in Paris, completed therefore around 1256. The *Summa Contra Gentiles (ScG)* was, according to Aquinas's biographer, written during the pontificate of Urban IV and therefore between 1261 and 1264. The *Summa Theologiae,* unfinished at his death, was written over the remaining years of his short life—Parts One and Two between 1265 and 1272, the unfinished Part Three in 1273, broken off at Question Ninety on the Sacrament of Penance.

Over his lifetime he also composed a number of smaller works, including commentaries on scripture, on Aristotle, and on other philosophers; academic disputations (the sort of "publish or perish" works of medieval university life); polemical attacks on other theologians and philosophers (also a staple of medieval university and ecclesiastical life); treatises and opinions on special subjects; theological letters; and devotional compositions and sermons. The songs of *Corpus Christi* would fit, obviously, into the last category and would have been composed, most likely, during the final stages of his work on *ScG,* but before the massive undertaking of *ST.*

His Importance

Aquinas remains, even today, over seven hundred and fifty years after his death, the most important of all Christian philosophers and theologians. But I think it is only now, thanks to the neo-Thomist revival of the early part of the twentieth century, that we can see clearly why. It is not so much because of what he says, but because of the full-scale re-orientation of the Christian mind that he pioneered. Again, one can only summarize the magnificent analyses of scholars like Pieper and Gilson and brilliant popularizers like Chesterton, but here it is.

What Aquinas brought to Christian thinking, and therefore to all Western thinking—at a crucial moment in its development—was a "radical inclusiveness." It was an inclusiveness partially due to his lifelong encounter with Aristotle, and a radicalism largely due to his whole-hearted commitment to the "evangelicalism" of the Dominican order. And in both areas, Thomas joined highly suspect and mostly anti-establishment movements.

One papal decree after another condemned the study of the great pagan philosopher, and yet the great universities outside the reach of papal power advertised for students by promising them the forbidden Aristotle. The state University of Naples, where Thomas began his serious studies, was one of those rebellious seats of learning; and there Aquinas first came into contact with the ideas of Aristotelian radicals like Michael Scot and Peter Ireland. His master in Paris and Cologne, Albert the Great, was the premiere Aristotelian of his generation, and time and again master and protégé studied and published Aristotelian works. And what drew medieval master and student irresistibly to this great ancient philosopher-scientist was not that Aristotle was always right, but that Aristotle was always, unlike *his* master Plato, in firm contact with the real world. To quote Pieper: Aristotle, in Thomas Aquinas's view,

> refuses to withdraw from the realities present to the senses, refuses to be distracted from those things that are evident to the eyes. And Thomas himself emphatically accepted this principle. Here was the decisive turn to concreteness, to the empirical reality of the world. Those things evident to the senses, which can be seen, heard, tasted, smelled, and touched, are to be taken as realities in their own right, standing on their own ground—not as mere reflections, shadows, not as mere symbols of something else, something invisible, spiritual, other-worldly. (p. 45)

Obvious as this may seem to us now, it was in his time radical. For the combined forces of Augustinianism and what Pieper calls Christian "spiritualistic symbolism" threatened to reduce all material creation to a totally shadow existence, leading to "a denaturalization of the natural world" which "sooner or later had to become intolerable; it is simply impossible to live a healthy and human life in a world populated exclusively by symbols" (p. 47).

The acceptance of the real world, and of the power and obligation of human reason to explore it, is what makes Aquinas's work inclusive. What makes him radical is his bold assertion that between the truth of reason and the truth of faith there must be, there can be, no conflict. What also makes him radical is his insistence on a return to Sacred Scripture in search of the truth of faith. This intellectual return to the bible was as startling in theological studies as the Dominican and Franciscan return to the gospel virtue of voluntary poverty was in the ascetic movement.

And what is further startling is that Thomas simultaneously embraced a spiritual life of radical material self-denial and an intellectual life of an all-inclusive acceptance of material reality. In other words, unlike earlier neo-Platonic asceticisms, his abnegation of the material world was not based on the belief that the material world was some kind of a shadow of an image of reality (as in Plato's cave), not really worth embracing in the first place, at worst a delusion, at best a weak symbol of spiritual reality; instead the reality and even the goodness of the material world were never denied, but one denied oneself some portion of the real pleasures of the real world for the sake of the equally real but higher spiritual world. It was, suggests Pieper, this fusion of an intellectual philosophy and a biblical theology in his personal life that compelled him to attempt the great synthesis of reason and faith which occupied every minute of his public life (p. 62). His success with this synthesis is the reason he is so important even today, and why, since his time, no Christian thinker has been able to look at his own world and his own faith except—at least partially—through Thomistic eyes.

The Feast of Corpus Christi

The sacrament of the Eucharist, in the sacrifice of the Mass, is the pivotal liturgical action of Catholic Christianity. As such it is a memorial re-enactment of the pivotal saving action of salvation history, the redemptive sacrifice of Jesus the Son of God on the Cross. But it is not just a memorial that celebrates a past event; it is, in the Catholic view, the actual re-creation of that event, caused by the sacramental fact that the offered bread and wine actually become the Body and Blood of the Savior ("This is my Body"). So the Eucharist, in classic theology, is primarily a real action, an event—not a static thing, certainly not just a symbol.

Because according to Catholic theology, "transubstantiation" occurs, Christ's Sacred Body and Blood are really present under the appearances of bread and wine. This doctrine of Real Presence—unique to Catholicism—

10

coupled with a reaction to Eucharistic controversies rampant in the Middle Ages, ultimately resulted in a growing "cult" of the Eucharist, in which the sacramental Presence became itself the object of worship and adoration *outside the context of the Mass.* Indeed by the thirteenth century, the Mass itself tended to be viewed, in the words of the *Catholic Encyclopedia,*

> as a dramatization of the Passion, as a kind of spectacle that one watched rather than participated in. The communion of the faithful, moreover had greatly declined by the 13th century, and thus looking upon the Host was for many a substitute for receiving the Eucharist. (*CE,* "Corpus Christi")

It is in this historical and theological context that we must view the establishment of the Feast of Corpus Christi.

The context may have been the twin influences of Eucharistic controversy and liturgical misperception, but the catalyst was a Belgian mystic and Augustinian nun named Julianna of Liège, whose vision of a moon partially obscured by a dark area, she interpreted as an image of the splendor of the Church blemished by the absence of a feast in honor of the Blessed Sacrament. She seems to have had an office for the feast compiled and composed by a fellow Augustinian as early as 1228; but it was not until 1247, through the influence of the Archdeacon of Liège, that the local bishop officially instituted such a feast in his diocese in 1247. From Belgium the practice quickly spread across northeastern Europe. And in 1264, by which time that Archdeacon had become Pope Urban IV, the feast was technically extended to the universal Church. Surprisingly, in spite of the original Papal Bull, the feast did not really catch on for another fifty or so years, when two later popes, Clement V and John XXII insisted on it. Thereafter the feast spread widely, and local offices for the feast multiplied, in some places replacing the original office from Liège, as well as the Roman office and the papally commissioned Thomistic office. What we have now is probably a fifteenth-century compilation of pieces from various offices, including (presumably) some of Thomas's own work.

One of the strongest proofs of Thomas's hand in the songs is their theology. For where one might expect, given the context of the commission, texts that yield to the popular static version of Sacramental devotion (the pietistic, subjective, uncritical looking-at-the-Host-in-awe version), one gets instead an aggressively active, perceptive, almost exhausting Sacramentalism, emphasizing again and again sacrificial and eating motifs, a theology drawn equally from scripture and philosophical speculation, and rooted firmly in the liturgy of the Mass, rather than the para-liturgy of Eucharistic processions and expositions.

The dominance of the procession in Corpus Christi celebrations brings me to one or two final observations. The first is that the offices and ceremonies for the feast do seem to mimic Holy Thursday liturgies, along with the expansion of the liturgical procession of Holy Week into a kind of religio-civic parade. And while the Thomistic texts emphasize the Last Supper aspects of the liturgy, the ensuing extra-liturgical celebrations through the centuries tended to replace theology with a combination of subjective piety and public-spiritedness, the latter becoming an occasion for public display and even playfulness.

This may be a legitimate cause for concern to a liturgist, but the student of Western Culture can only be grateful. For the celebration of Corpus Christi in the late spring, in good weather, had the effect of drawing the more public parts of the Easter celebration with it, especially those parts which had already begun their transformation into religious drama. And oddly enough, the Easter Alleluia seems to have been the common source for both the liturgical Sequence and the earliest liturgical plays; both came from the fitting of new words to the extended melody on the final "-a" of the Alleluia. The wonderful *Victimae Paschali Laudes* sequence of Easter is a kind of recapitulation of the movement from song to staging, with its transition into dramatic dialogue halfway through ("*Dic nobis Maria*"— "Tell us, Mary, what did you see?") (*MR*, p. 406).

As the liturgical plays of Easter began to outgrow their place in the Mass and to morph into the mystery cycles of the late Middle Ages; as they moved off the altar and out into the square, and out of the hands of the clergy and into the control of the guilds; as they became massive civic events, both stationary and processional, the Easter weather was no longer dependable enough to risk the outlay of funds and energy, and so the cycles moved to this new feast day, celebrated in warmer weather, and thus became the "Corpus Christi plays"—the most important predecessors of the great humanist and secular drama of the Renaissance. Thus, but for Julianna's visions of the spotted moon in her Belgian cloister, we might have missed not only the songs of Aquinas but the plays of Shakespeare as well.

The Songs of the Church

Of all the forms of Church singing, only two need concern us here—the hymn and the sequence, for Thomas's songs fall only into those two categories. But in order to understand and appreciate his songs fully, one must know a little of the history and the development of these two forms.

The **Sequence** is the more recent of the two, first surfacing in the ninth century. The word "sequence" seems initially to have been used to describe the melodic, but not textual, expansion of the Alleluia verse in the Mass; in this context, the words "*jubilus*" makes its appearance in the writings of a ninth-century liturgical writer named Amalarius, who reported that singers were now calling the Alleluia "*jubilus*" a "sequence."

But the first really extensive treatment came from a Swiss monk named Nokter who, in a prefatory letter to his collection of songs, described his difficulty remembering all the melodic cadences of the various Alleluia jubilations and so resorted to a mnemonic trick he was taught by a visiting monk from a French abbey: the practice of laying a text under the melody. This device, with the various words keyed to the various pitches of the melody, not only helped Notker remember the cadences, it gave him, he says, the idea of composing texts specifically for the melodies; and after a few tries, and some help from his teacher, he developed his own style—a completely syllabic text (one syllable per note), with the sense of the words perfectly keyed to the rise and fall of the music. Eventually he published a set of these, under the title, *A Book of Hymns*.

But his word "hymn" did not stick; and his new invention, the "sequence," remained for a while undeveloped. Gradually, the texts moved into a more poetic, rather than prosaic, form. Rhyme and meter were introduced, and eventually a rather strict stanzaic structure. Simultaneously, the melodies became more complex. Unlike the Hymn, which used a single melody for all the verses, the Sequence used some variation of a series of paired melodies and verses arranged in a complex chain, building often toward a grand climax.

In other words, without ever losing its dominantly syllabic form or its direct relation to the Mass, it took on a life of its own and was no longer merely a melodic or textual expansion of the Alleluia. It became an enormously popular form, with thousands of sequences being written; and in the hands of brilliant artists like Wipo, who wrote the astonishingly beautiful Easter sequence *Victimae Pascali Laudes*; Adam of St. Victor, who perfected the middle style; and Thomas Aquinas, who wrote in the late style, the sequence became one of the most prolific and important forms of church song for hundreds of years.

A backlash was probably inevitable, and amidst its many reformations, the Council of Trent in the sixteenth century eliminated from the liturgy all but four sequences, Wipo's Easter Sequence, Aquinas's Corpus Christi Sequence, the Pentecost Sequence *Veni Sancte Spiritus* (variously ascribed either to Innocent III or to Stephen Langton, the Archbishop of Canterbury), and the wonderful *Dies Irae* (perhaps by Thomas a Celano) in the Mass for the Dead. In 1727, a fifth sequence, the thirteenth-century *Stabat Mater* (perhaps by Jacopone da Todi) was re-introduced for the Feast of the Seven Sorrows.

Hymns have a much longer history. They go back certainly as far as St. Ambrose of Milan—St. Augustine's mentor—in the fifth century. The legend has it that Ambrose—ever since acknowledged as the father of Latin hymnody—began writing his beautiful, theologically packed songs in response to the Arian heretics in his diocese, who were themselves using music and poetry in the service of their doctrinal agenda. Ambrose's hymns were popular and eminently singable, and it was not long before they became a staple of the liturgy. And soon after that, they and other hymns written in the Ambrosian style were incorporated into the Office as well, that set of hourly prayers and readings—both sung and spoken—required of the Catholic clergy for centuries.

So the two essential differences between hymns and sequences is that a hymn uses a single melody for all its verses, and that a hymn is not, and did not begin as, an integral part of the Mass.

The Poetic Structure of the Verse

There is one further thing that makes the study of hymns particularly complex for the scholar or singer: their long history meant that the hymns, unlike the sequences, were more subject to the major revolutions in Latin poetics that marked the move from the very early Middle Ages to the early Renaissance. To understand this is to appreciate the difficulties of translating Thomas's hymns accurately and still making them singable to the current liturgical melodies.

This is a complicated subject, and I refer the reader to Joseph Connelly's magisterial *Hymns of the Roman Liturgy* for a fuller treatment, of which I present a brief summary here.

When Ambrose wrote, the dominant metrical scheme of the educated Latin poets was what scholars call "quantitative." For those of us raised in the English language and on English poetry, this is a difficult concept to grasp. Essentially, it means that—unlike most of the poetry we are familiar with—the guiding principle of Latin metrical verse was not accent or stress, and certainly not rhyme—but the length or shortness of the syllables— simply stated, the relative measure of time it took (theoretically and really) to pronounce the sounds of a string of syllables. A regular alternation of long and short syllables—rather than stressed and unstressed syllables— created the various meters traditionally called "classical."

Even in Ambrose's day, this was a difficult concept for the people to grasp, and—if the hymns were to be popular—it was almost impossible to put into practice. The people apparently responded—as we do now—to accent rather than length. And so Ambrose, a classicist, made a compromise; he chose a classical meter that allowed him almost always to align the long syllables with the accented ones. And what began as quantitative with traces of accentual gradually mutated over the centuries until it became accentual with traces of quantitative; and then even the quantitative traces disappeared. At least they did until the unhappy reforms of the High Renaissance, when the great humanist Pope Urban VIII insisted the hymnal be revised to fit newly rediscovered classical quantitative standards, and many of the great hymns were unfortunately "disimproved" (See Connelly, pp. xvii–xviii).

The other change in Latin poetry occurred at the ends of lines. Faced with the difficulty of making verse communally singable, and therefore with the need to leave or create regular pauses for breath, it became necessary to find a way not just to end the sense at the end of each breath line—not necessary in classical meters—but also somehow to mark the end of each breath line sonically. Accentually, one could not dependably do it by landing heavily on the last syllable of a line, because Latin had no polysyllables accented on the last syllable. And the quantitative technique of a long final syllable was no longer a practical solution in the now accentually structured hymns. Enter, therefore, rhyme, which created the necessary sound closure at the end of each breath line.

The traditional hymns of the Catholic Church, therefore, ultimately became primarily accentual, rhymed compositions to be sung to familiar melodies. The difficulty is that, upon occasion, when new texts were composed for old melodies, there might still be a battle between the quantitative thrust of the old melodies and the accentual structure of the new lyrics. We find this to be true in some of the songs of Aquinas, when, for example his accentual lyrics for the Corpus Christi *Pange Lingua* are set against the mostly quantitative melodies of an older Holy Week *Pange Lingua* (by another author) which served as its model. And there is, as well, something of a quantitative bias in plainchant as well, one that permits the near stressing of final syllables, especially those with extended cadences over them. The singing of Aquinas's *Pange Lingua,* after all—as anyone who has ever sung it must admit—traditionally goes something like this (boldface indicating stress, dots indicating number of notes per syllable):

>   ..   ..
> *Pange lingua gloriosi*
>   ..   ...
> *Corporis mysterium, etc.*

The result is that unstressed syllables like "*-gua*" and "*-um*" end up getting an unavoidable stress because of the length of time it takes to sing their multiple notes.

English does not adapt particularly well to this phenomenon, especially in those cases where we find the Latin sung accent apparently shifting position from one verse to the next. Look, for example at the last lines of the first two verses of the *Lauda Sion.* They are meant to be sung to the same melody, yet their accentual patterns are completely different:

> *In hymnis et canticis*
> *Nec laudare sufficis.*

The result is that the first line is almost inevitably rendered, as once again all singers will recognize:

In *hymnis* **et canticis.**

I point out this phenomenon, only to offer some explanation why my translations on the page may read unmetrically or awkwardly. They are not meant to obey the strict rules of either quantitative or accentual meters; they are meant to fit the melodies to which they are traditionally sung.

The Structure of This Study

Which brings us to the final topic of this introduction: the nature of this little book. It is primarily a translation of the four Thomistic songs, with accompanying commentary. I have undertaken this task, really, for three simple reasons: because I love these songs, because I want to hear them sung again in church, and because the English fragments of them that are now represented in the popular hymnals and mass-books of today's Church are mostly out of date and occasionally misrepresentations, lacking—even when not totally inaccurate—the depth and subtlety and sheer daring of Aquinas's poetry.

Let me give one example, from the *Panis Angelicus.* This song, as it is commonly sung today, actually consists of the final two verses of St. Thomas's magnificent *Sacris Solemniis,* his hymn for Matins of the feast. When we sing it today out of the missalette—for example, out of the one currently used in my own musically very sophisticated parish—the words of the third and fourth lines of the next to last verse go like this:

> We humble people come to eat your sacred food,
> In peace, joy, love, and gratitude. (*Missalette*, p. 110)

What Thomas actually wrote is:

> *O res mirabilis! Manducat Dominum*
> *Pauper, servus, et humilis.*

Connelly translates this as:

> What marvelous happening is this; the poor, the servant, the lowly feeds upon his Lord. (p. 122)

The missalette version (credited to Jerome Siweck, 1986) completely omits any attempt at translating the first section *"O res mirabilis"* (O wondrous thing). So obviously Connelly's translation is more accurate here, though (unfortunately) it is just barely English. First of all, "happening" is a poor choice for *"res"* (simply "thing" would be better); perhaps he chooses the gerund ("-ing") because it allows, but hardly justifies, the absence of any article (like "a" or "the") in the English. This may slavishly represent the Latin—which has no such article—but hardly does justice to the English meaning, which in all probability requires one. "What an amazing thing!" would be so much simpler and more accurate—both in expression and emotion.

As for the second sentence, there is no "peace," "joy," "love," or "gratitude" in the original, and the "humble" is a serious misreading of the more socially minded *"humilis"* ("low-born") of the Latin; so the missalette version is not even a paraphrase. Connelly's translation is again closer, though "his" has no equivalent in the Latin; and even more barbarously, English adjectival substantives like "the poor" and "the lowly" cannot take a singular verb (like "feeds"), though Latin adjectival substantives can. So syntactically "The poor, the servant, the lowly feeds upon his Lord" is fatally flawed. "The poor, the enslaved, the low-born feed on the Lord" would be better, but still misses two important connotations. The first is the physicality of *"manducat"*; of all the words Thomas might have chosen, he picks the one that emphasizes the teeth and the act of chewing—"masticate" might be closer; not for the faint of heart is Thomas's theology. The second connotation is the wordplay on *"Dominus,"* which means, of course "lord" and therefore "Our Lord," but also means—in the context of dining—"the master of the feast," or simply, "the host." English cannot make the equivalent wordplay (Lord-Master), though "feast on the host"—with a substitute wordplay (Master-Host)—might be serendipitously acceptable.

Finally, we might suspect that the Latin wordplay is exactly what Thomas had in mind because his verses echo the Vulgate version of

Matthew's parable of the dinner invitations (Mt 14:15–24). Jesus introduces His story with the phrase: "Blessed is he who will dine"—literally, "will chew bread," (*manducabit panem*)—"in the kingdom of God." Then the familiar parable proceeds to tell of a master (*dominus*) who, upon receiving excuses from his invited guests, orders a servant (*servus*) to round up the poor (*pauperi*), the sick, the blind, and the lame from the highways and byways to take their places at the table. This would be indeed an amazing feast; and clearly Thomas thought of it as a model for the Eucharistic Feast, not just in the disproportion between the food and the feeders, but also in the displacement of the original invitees by the new guests—that is, the displacement and simultaneous fulfillment of the Old Covenant Passover meal by the New Pasch—a constant theme of the *Corpus Christi* songs.

Now that we know what Thomas actually wrote and clearly alluded to, the missalette translation leaves us seriously starved for nourishment. None of the biblical echoes are there, none of the social and theological daring, none of the paradox, none of the wordplay, none of the aggressive liturgical context of the Sacred Supper. Instead, we get the very Eucharistic attitude that Thomas seems to have deliberately excluded from his song—the passive, personal (rather than communal) attitude toward the Host as a thing almost too grand to be approached ("in peace, joy, love, and gratitude"), rather than our common daily spiritual chewable heavenly bread.

What I have tried to illustrate with this one example is that the songs can be so much richer than current translations might lead us to suspect. In fact, they are—I confess!—untranslatably rich, if one accepts the burden of being faithful to form as well as content. Accurate rhymes, precise connotations, the amazing density of expression, and the burden of fitting the words to extant melodies may simply not be attainable in English. Thus, my work—if it is not to fail completely—must include more than a translation. What I have done—in addition to singable translations—is to provide the reader with accurate explications and appreciations primarily of the Latin text of the Sequence, as well as commentary on some of the biblical, philosophical, and theological references embedded in it. Then I have moved on to his three hymns, with somewhat shorter commentaries.

To do this, I have depended largely on Thomas's own work as a source of enlightenment—primarily, his *Summa Theologiae*. What emerges from all this is a kind of unstructured summary of Aquinas's Eucharistic theology, presented not in a systematic but in a freer form, in which each verse or line or even phrase of the various songs may become an occasion for a deeper meditation, an associative digression, a kind of joyous exploration into deeper meaning. In short, this book itself, like its subject, is meant to be no less than a *jubilatio mentis,* an alleluia of the mind.

The Sequence

Lauda Sion Salvatorem
By Thomas Aquinas

Praise the Savior, Zion, Sing
Translation by Dakin Matthews

Lauda Sion Salvatórem
Lauda ducem et pastórem
In hymnis et cánticis.
Quantum potes, tantum aude:
Quia major omni laude,
Nec laudáre súfficis.

Laudis thema speciális,
Panis vivus et vitális,
Hódie propónitur.
Quem in sacræ mensa cœnæ,
Turbæ fratrum duodénæ
Datum non ambígitur.

Sit laus plena, sit sonóra,
Sit jucúnda, sit decóra
Mentis jubilátio.
Dies enim solémnis ágitur,
In qua mensæ prima recólitur
Hujus institútio.

In hac mensa novi Regis,
Novum Pascha novæ legis,
Phase vetus términat.
Vetustátem nóvitas,
Umbram fugat véritas,
Noctem lux elíminat.

Quod in cœna Christus gessit,
Faciéndum hoc expréssit
In sui memóriam.
Docti sacris institútis,

Praise the Savior, Zion, sing;
Praise the shepherd, praise the king
In your hymns and holy chants.
Let your praise be bold as can be,
You can never praise sufficiently,
He transcends all utterance.

And today we have proposed to us
A theme for praise most glorious:
Bread of Life, the Living Bread,
At that Holy Supper given out,
A fact which we must never doubt,
On which Twelve Apostles fed.

Let your praise be full and sounding,
Pleasing, proper, and redounding,
From a soul that's jubilant.
For we celebrate today a solemn feast,
That recalls the meal at which our
Savior-Priest
First gave us this Sacrament.

On this table of the new King,
The new Passover offering
Frees the Old Law of its hold.
Then the truth puts shadows to flight
Then the daylight conquers the night,
And the new dispels the old.

What Christ at that supper did then
He ordered to be done again,
In His sacred memory.
His holy orders we now obey,

Panem, vinum, in salútis
Consecrámus hóstiam.

We consecrate the host today—
Bread and wine that sets us free.

Dogma datur Christiánis,
Quod in carnem transit panis,
Et vinum in sánguinem.
Quod non capis, quod non vides,
Animósa firmat fides,
Præter rerum ordinem.

This is part of our Christian creed:
That bread becomes His flesh indeed,
And wine becomes His blood as well.
What you cannot see or perceive,
Fervent faith can help you believe,
Far beyond what's natural.

Sub divérsis speciébus,
Signis tantum, et non rebus,
Latent res exímiæ.
Caro cibus, sanguis potus:
Manet tamen Christus totus,
Sub utráque spécie.

Underneath two different figurings—
Only signs, and not really things,
Lie unique realities.
His blood to drink, His flesh to eat;
Yet is Christ the Lord complete,
Under either shape one sees.

A suménte non concísus,
Non confráctus, non divísus:
Integer accípitur.
Sumit unus, sumunt mille:
Quantum isti, tantum ille:
Nec sumptus consúmitur.

He gives Himself for our nourishment,
Not divided, broken, or rent,
He is consumed whole, complete.
Each one receives as much as all,
Christ is inexhaustible,
Whether one or thousands eat.

Sumunt boni, sumunt mali:
Sorte tamen inæquáli,
Vitæ vel intéritus.
Mors est malis, vita bonis:
Vide paris sumptiónis
Quam sit dispar éxitus.

Good and bad alike may receive,
The good will joy, the bad will grieve,
So unlike, the fates they meet.
Life to the good, but death to the bad,
See what diverse ends may be had
From the same food that they eat.

Fracto demum Sacraménto,
Ne vacílles, sed memento,
Tantum esse sub fragménto,
Quantum toto tégitur.

After all the breaking is done,
Each part holds as much as one;
This remember and do not shun
A sliver of the Sacrament.

24

Nulla rei fit scissúra:
Signi tantum fit fractúra:
Qua nec status nec statúra
Signáti minúitur.

Ecce panis Angelórum,
Factus cibus viatórum:
Vere panis filiórum,
Non mitténdus cánibus.
In figúris præsignátur,
Cum Isaac immolátur:
Agnus paschæ deputátur
Datur manna pátribus.

Bone pastor, panis vere,
Jesu, nostri miserére:
Tu nos pasce, nos tuére:
Tu nos bona fac vidére
In terra vivéntium.
Tu, qui cuncta scis et vales:
Qui nos pascis hic mortáles:
Tuos ibi commensáles,
Cohærédes et sodáles,
Fac sanctórum cívium.

Amen. Allelúja.

No reality is broken,
What is split is just a token,
But the thing which is bespoken
Suffers no diminishment.

This is truly Angels's bread,
Giv'n to earthly pilgrims instead;
On such bread are children fed,
It is not cast away on curs.
It is prefigured by the ram,
That spares the son of Abraham,
By the slaughter of the Paschal lamb,
By manna giv'n our forefathers.

Loving Shepherd, O Lord Jesus,
Living Bread, have mercy on us,
Lead us, feed us, Lord, and bring us,
To see all things glorious,
In the land of the living.
You that know and ground the
universe,
Feeder here of mortal travelers,
Make us there your table-sharers,
Comrades and co-inheritors
With the saints in heaven.

Amen. Alleluia.

INTRODUCTION TO THE *SUMMA*

Reading the *Summa Theologiae* can be very frustrating for the modern theologian because sometimes Aquinas seems overly concerned with questions that we no longer care about. (But then, that was the theology of his day, and the *Summa* was meant to be an exhaustive reference book for scholars of theology; so it tried to cover *everything*, especially how to unravel the doctrinal intricacies of the faith and persuasively answer challenges to them.) Also, the theology of his time had adopted a complex jargon of its own, a private language almost, which can be extremely confusing and off-putting almost eight centuries later, well after the demise of Medieval Latin. Also, Thomas's theological analyses are often constructed on philosophical premises that we no longer consider viable or valuable or even true; so there's that. And also, I think, it is because his *method* of argument is so foreign to us. If you've never experienced it, here's a brief snapshot of that method:

He starts with a general **Topic**, like "The Eucharist."

Then he isolates one area of that topic, called a "**Question**"—for example, "The Sacrament Itself," which he briefly describes in a **Prologue**.

Next, he proposes a single, narrow statement about the "Question" called an "**Article**" (which will in fact turn out to be the opposite of what he actually believes)—such as "The Eucharist seems not to be a Sacrament."

Then he lists one or more arguments **seeming to support** that proposition; sometimes these are just quotations from other theologians or liturgy or scripture, sometimes they are actual arguments.

Then he lists usually a single statement **seeming to oppose** that proposition.

Then he gives his "**Answer**," in opposition to the original statement.

27

Then one by one, he refutes the "supporting" arguments, called his "**Responses.**"

Then he moves on to the next narrow "Article."

And when he's done with all the "Articles" in a particular "Question," he moves on to the next "Question" in the "Topic," again subdividing it into "Articles."

And so on.

It's not what we would call a holistic approach, but one that seeks to conquer by dividing and subdividing.

In the multi-volume *Summa Theologiae*, the "Topic" of the Eucharist is covered in Questions 73 to 83—eleven in all—in the Third Part. The simplest way to cite a passage of the *Summa* is with three numbers, the first for the Part, the second for the Question, the third for the Article. (Some citations go deeper and get more complex, but for his writings on the Eucharist, the simpler version is sufficient.) Thus, for example, the very first Article on the Eucharist would be *ST* 3.83.1—*Summa Theologiae*, Part 3, Question 83, Article 1. (The translation I use is online and prepared by the Fathers of the English Dominican Province.)

The Eucharistic Doctrine in the *Summa*

Now in this very first Article, Aquinas makes a distinction that is crucial to his entire theology of the Eucharist; but, oddly, he does not do so in the body of his Answer, but tucked away in one of the early arguments supporting the proposition he disagrees with and then in his response to it. (This is probably because it is ground he has already covered extensively in earlier Questions on the Sacraments in general.)

Here he identifies three interconnected levels in the Eucharist, as he does in other sacraments. He has already proven (in *ST* 3.63 and 66) that every sacrament is composed of a sacred sign and a reality (*sacramentum et res*). The *baptismal* sign is the pouring of the water (*sacramentum*); the spiritual reality is the soul's new "character" of being reborn in Christ (*res*), but that "character"—here in *ST* 3.73.1—is also a spiritual sign and cause (*sacramentum*) of the cleansing of the soul of sin, the deeper reality (*res*). For the Eucharist, there is a similar tripartite division: the visible sign is clearly the appearance of bread and wine (*sacramentum*), and the reality is the actual presence of Christ's Body and Blood (*res*); yet for Aquinas, Christ's true body (the Real Presence) is not just a reality (*res*) but is also itself a sacred sign (*sacramentum*) of another deeper reality (another *res*)— Christ's Mystical Body, the saving union of all believers in Him.

Also tucked away in one of the early sections of the Article is another important observation by Aquinas—that the Eucharist, like the other Sacraments, is a Sacrament of the "New Law." This allows him to continuously look back to the "Old Law" or the "Old Covenant" for anticipations of the Eucharist, which he finds enormously important, not only because of the "fulfillment and replacement" theme with regards to the Eucharist, but also because it satisfies his love of analogous argumentation—his sense that resemblances provide a kind of persuasive unity. "The spiritual life," he observes, again in this first Article, "is analogous to the corporeal life, since corporeal things bear a resemblance to the spiritual."

And then in the Answer section ("*Respondeo*"), Aquinas provides a third building block of his Eucharistic doctrine, perhaps even the keystone, that the Eucharist is first and foremost "food" for man's spiritual life, just as bread and wine are food for his material life.

These three ideas, that the Eucharist is essentially food; that it is a replacement and fulfillment of something in the Old Covenant; and that what is most deeply signified by the Eucharist is the saving union of all believers in Christ's Mystical Body (thus the alternate name, *communio*, the "union with" all the other members in Christ)—these are three ideas which dominate the theology of his songs. The three levels of signification link the Eucharist with the past (commemorating Christ's sacrifice on the cross), the present (Christ's actual presence, unifying the celebrators of the sacrament), and the future (life everlasting as members of Christ's Mystical Body at the end of our journey). Its place as a Sacrament of the "New Law" allows him to mine the "Old Covenant" for prefigurings and deeper understandings. And his insistence on its being "food" resolutely identifies the Eucharist as something primarily to be taken and eaten, and not simply adored in awe at a distance.

Aquinas's prose antiphon for Vespers on Corpus Christi "*O Sacrum Convivium*" is perhaps a perfect example of how he combined the three approaches in a single sentence:

O sacrum convivium!
in quo Christus sumitur:
recolitur memoria passionis eius:
mens impletur gratia:
et futurae gloriae nobis pignus datur.

(B, *Vespers, Office of Corpus Christi*)

O sacred banquet,
In which Christ is eaten,
The memory of His passion is re-celebrated,
The soul is filled with grace,
And we are given a pledge of future glory.

(*Translation mine*)

The first two lines assert that is it a communal meal in which the food is truly Christ Himself. It looks to the past, present, and future.

To the **past** event of Christ's passion, which it not only recalls, but "memorializes"; "*recolitur*" is something stronger than simply "is remembered," because the "memory" itself is already expressed in the word "*memoria.*" Something further is *done with* that memory, something more than just remembering it; in a sense the memory is re-activated, re-celebrated, even re-realized, perhaps. ("*Do this*, in memory of me"—not "Have this memory of me.")

It looks to the **present** because Christ is truly present at that moment and because the celebrants are thereby "in communion" with Him; and also because of the first immediate effect of the Sacrament on the receiver, which Aquinas identifies as the filling of the soul with grace to the extent that the Eucharist bestows upon that soul a new "character" (*ST* 3.79.1 and *ST* 3.63.1).

It looks to the "**future** glory" of the perfection of the Mystical Body by the union of all saved souls under their Head, the risen Christ, and simultaneously gives a "pledge" (*pignus*, literally "a pawn" of that "glory")—something more than a verbal promise, something real like a down payment, which is simultaneously a foretaste of future glory and the means by which we are refreshed on our journey towards that final end (thus,

Aquinas's firm approval of an alternate name for the Eucharist "Viaticum")—what we take with us to feed us on the way (*ST* 3.79.2).

So now we begin our exploration of the Lauda Sion *verse by verse—fourteen sections in all (some verses being too rich for a single section). In these sections are analyses and explications of the Latin text, comments on the poetry, doctrinal references to the Summa, scriptural allusions, explanations of my translation choices, even personal comments on my appreciation of and reaction to the verse.*

For those so inclined, they may even serve as occasions for two weeks' worth of daily meditations. If they lead to prayer, they justify their sometimes rambling nature.

First Verse

Lauda Sion Salvatórem
Lauda ducem et pastórem
  In hymnis et cánticis.
Quantum potes, tantum aude:
Quia major omni laude,
  Nec laudáre súfficis.

Praise the Savior, Zion, sing;
Praise the shepherd, praise the king
  In your hymns and holy chants.
Let your praise be bold as can be,
You can never praise sufficiently,
  He transcends all utterance.

    In this first verse, Aquinas demands that the Church praise its Savior, Leader, and Shepherd in song. And he further insists that she be bold about it, as daring as she can be, because no praise will ever be sufficient, as Christ is greater than all praise.

    The use of the word "*Sion*," or "Zion," is simultaneously a look to the *past* (the Jerusalem of the Old Covenant, where praises were ritually offered); a glance at the *present* (to the celebrating Church itself on the occasion of the feast and to the fulfillment of the promise to the Chosen People in Christ); and a glimpse of the *future* (the Heavenly Jerusalem of the world to come). Thus the familiar "past, present, and future" meanings of the Eucharist are introduced in a single word at the very beginning.

    In the liturgy, Christ is often identified by a triple title—one of the most common being King/Prophet/Priest. Yet here, Aquinas chooses a different configuration: Savior/Leader/Shepherd. I think this is mostly because these three titles are most appropriate for this Sacrament. The sacrifice of the Cross memorialized in the Eucharistic is the "saving event" of human history. Christ Himself is the "leader," or, as we shall see, more accurately the Head of the Mystical Body, of which the believers are the members and co-heirs of His glory—thus avoiding the monarchical connotations of a king (*rex*) who "rules his subjects" and preferring the more benevolent connotations of a shepherd (*pastor*) who "leads his sheep." And the Eucharistic "bread and wine" are the spiritual food (*pastor* literally meaning "feeder").

Sadly in my translation, for the sake of rhyme, I could not avoid the word "king" nor honor Aquinas's preferred order of the titles; and thus it is that any translation that tries to honor both the form and content of the original is likely to fall short; and the first verse also becomes a fruitful exercise in humility for the translator, trying to do all he can and necessarily being insufficient to the task. An experience which echoes the verse itself.

It is in the second sub-stanza (the last three lines), that I find perhaps the most striking observation in the first verse. Here, as I suggested earlier, Thomas avoids the reticence of St. Augustine when it comes to talking about the "inexpressible" Godhead. Where Augustine may seem at times to find God's "total otherness," His inexpressible Divine Nature, to be a discouragement and a warning against trying to say too much, Aquinas takes it as an encouragement, a challenge even, to say everything you possibly can, with the full knowledge you can never say enough. Connelly points out that this is pretty much a re-statement of Ecclesiasticus 43.29–33 (p. 125).

This is also, I think, not a bad summary of Thomas's attitude towards not just songs of praise, but to the entire enterprise of his theology. Do everything in your power. Fearlessly. If we believe the famous legend, there may come a time when it will all seem just so much "straw"; but until that time comes, harvest as much as you can and offer it to others. "Contemplata aliis tradere" is, after all, the motto, derived from his writings, of Aquinas' beloved Dominican order.

Verse Two

Laudis thema speciális,
Panis vivus et vitális,
  Hódie propónitur.
Quem in sacræ mensa cœnæ,
Turbæ fratrum duodénæ
  Datum non ambígitur.

And today we have proposed to us
A theme for praise most glorious:
  Bread of Life, the Living Bread,
At that Holy Supper given out,
A fact which we must never doubt,
  On which Twelve Apostles fed.

Having in the first verse urged the Church to sing the praises of the Lord, Aquinas now identifies the *particular* theme of "special praise" for the day, thus tying the Sequence to the feast of Corpus Christi—"The Bread of Life, the Living Bread." And specifically he ties it to the reality of the physical "table" of the Last Supper. In this way, he narrows the focus of the feast not so much to the mere *existence* of the Eucharist, as to its *place and function in salvation history*, which starts with anchoring it simultaneously in the past and the present—the *past* because of the "historical fact" of the Last Supper, when the Twelve Apostles, as a group, were given the "Bread of Life"; and the *present* because that "Bread" is still living and giving life (*vivus et vitalis*) and also because today (*hodie*)—which is any day on which the feast is celebrated—that reality is ever to be praised and never to be doubted. As real as a table (*mensa*). (In *ST* 3.75.1 Aquinas cites Hilary as saying "There is no room for doubt regarding the truth of Christ's body and blood.")

In my translation, I have added some first person plurals ("us, we") that are not explicit in the original—though they are certainly understood; a proposal (*proponitur*) and a doubt (*dubitur*) surely involve people who are receiving the proposal and people who can harbor the doubt. And the Church ("Zion") is surely a collective, a crowd even (*turba*), as the Twelve

34

were. So the plurality of the those called to praise and warned not to doubt matches the plurality of the Apostles at the table of the holy supper (*sacrae mensa caenae*).

I would like to think that these plurals, both explicit and understood, reflect one of Aquinas's central truths about the Eucharist—that it is not a private, individual devotion, but a shared meal that unifies us all into the Body of Christ, even as we consume the Body of Christ. As Aquinas notes in another article in this Question, citing Augustine: "Nor shalt thou change Me into thyself, as food of thy flesh, but thou shalt be changed into Me" (*ST* 3.73.3). And what the Eucharistic most essentially seems to celebrate is this "collective" transformation, this "communion" of all the members with one another under the Head. *Ut unum sint.* Perhaps this is also why both here and in his *Pange lingua*, Aquinas uses the Latin word for "brothers" (*fratrum, fratribus*) to describe the Twelve, not just because they were close to Jesus, but also because by their Eucharistic unity with Him, they could be co-heirs with Him, newmade "sons of God," and therefore truly "brothers" of the divine Christ.

By the way, this crowd of twelve brothers (turbae fratrum duodenae), to whom was given (datum) that first Eucharist, included, of course, Judas Iscariot; and Aquinas devotes an entire Article to the question of "Whether Christ gave His body to Judas?" (ST 3.81.2). His answer is an unequivocal yes; and the reasons why he thinks it was proper for Christ to do so are both complex and surprising. And instructive.

Verse Three

Sit laus plena, sit sonóra,
Sit jucúnda, sit decóra
  Mentis jubilátio.
Dies enim solémnis ágitur,
In qua mensæ prima recólitur
  Hujus institútio.

Let your praise be full and sounding,
Pleasing, proper, and redounding,
  From a soul that's jubilant.
For we celebrate today a solemn feast,
That recalls the meal at which our Savior-Priest
  First gave us this Sacrament.

It is from this verse that I drew the title of my study, though sadly in the translation itself I could not find a way to use the title—that wonderful third line: "*Mentis jubilatio*"—an "Alleluia of the mind." For more on that, and on the first three lines in general, I refer you back to the first few pages of the Introduction.

Here, let us ponder the last three lines. There are, I think, four expressions in the Latin worth unpacking further. One is the use of the phrase "this table" (*huius mensae*) for the expected "this Sacrament" (*huius sacramenti*). It is of course metonymy, the figure of speech that identifies something by some attribute or adjunct for that thing. Metonymy is very common in poetry, so it's not surprising; but to my ear it keeps grounding the sacrament in a physical reality. And in two ways.

First, I remember in my earliest experience in philosophy class with Aristotelian metaphysics, a "table" was, for some reason, the preferred piece of reality that was inevitably used to illustrate the difference between matter and form, and sometime substance and accidents. The metonymic use of the very real "table" for the somewhat abstract "Sacrament" always strikes me as a strategy not just to link today's altar with a crucial piece of furniture in the Upper Room (joining past and present, and reminding us that a meal is involved), but to insist on the hard reality of Christ's presence at the table both then and now.

And the other way, of course, is that the very point of poetry's use of such figures, almost the very point of poetry itself, is to make the abstract concrete, to return the concept back to the hearer the way it first came to the speaker. If nothing reaches the intellect except through the senses, as Thomas famously insisted (following his master Aristotle), then when communicating ideas (*contemplata tradere*) back to others (*aliis*), especially to other listeners or readers (or singers) who are not scholars, there's nothing quite so useful as re-incorporating the abstract back into something like the specific concrete image by which information is first received—sensible specificity.

The next memorable phase is "*prima institutio*" (the "first institution")—which is admittedly a kind of redundancy, since the act of instituting something is always a "first." So "*prima*" is more of an intensifier, I think; and the point of the intensification is to stress the ongoing nature of the sacramental act (*prima* as the first of a series). Again, there is a kind of poetic compression here; the meaning is not that there will be a second and third institution, but there will be, after the initial instituting sacramental act, second and third "re-enactments" of the Sacrament, continuing commemoratory performances of it.

And here we get to "*recolitur*." This is usually translated as "remembered" or "recalled" (as I have translated it in the hymn). But I prefer to think that Aquinas the poet, always aware of richer connotations, has more in mind by the use of this word than simple memory. Etymologically, it is derived from the Latin verb *colere*, which meant "to reside or inhabit or dwell," so perhaps there is also the idea of having the Last Supper not just "remembered" but "re-lived." Further, "*colere*" was a verb commonly used to describe the act of worship ("cult" is a derivation of it); so equally evoked by "*recolitur*" is the idea of "re-celebration," not just "memory" but "commemoration, memorialization." (See my earlier analyses of "*O Sacrum Convivium*" in the "Introduction to the *Summa*.")

And then we have "*agitur*" (is done, is acted). So not just "this is a solemn day" (*dies solemnis*), but a solemn day is "enacted"; the feast day doesn't just exist, it *does* something. *We* do something on it.

I close by noting that Aquinas's use of the technical term "institutio" should remind us that it was and is a critical doctrine to the Church that all seven sacraments were "instituted" by Christ. And that doctrine was one of the inflection points in the Protestant/Catholic split. An entire Article in the Summa is dedicated to the topic "Whether the institution of this sacrament was appropriate" (ST 3.73.5); and another on "Whether the sacraments were solely of divine institution" (ST 3.64.2).

Verse Four

In hac mensa novi Regis,
Novum Pascha novæ legis,
  Phase vetus términat.
Vetustátem nóvitas,
Umbram fugat véritas,
  Noctem lux elíminat.

On this table of the new King,
The new Passover offering
  Frees the Old Law of its hold.
Then the truth puts shadows to flight
Then the daylight conquers the night,
  And the new dispels the old.

Again the "table"—especially the dinner table—makes its physical pres-
ence felt! The first three lines, I admit, are quite loosely translated in my
version; rhymes require a certain amount of freedom. Connelly's literal
translation goes:

At the table of the new King, the new law's new pasch puts an
end to the old pasch. (p. 124)

Though the Latin has no articles and it is sometimes hard to choose between
"a" and "the" in this case—with the very definite "*hac*" ("this")—it's hard
to argue with the use of the definite "the" over the indefinite "a." "*Phase*" is
an alternate Latin word for "Passover." Aquinas's use of two separate words
was probably intended to highlight the difference between the old and the
new, especially as the more familiar "*Pascha*" was strongly associated with
Easter.

This is the first appearance of "king" (*regis*) in the sequence, perhaps
because so much emphasis in this verse is on the replacement of an old law
by a new, a power typically reserved to kings. And of course, by the New
and Old Law, we are to understand the New and Old Covenant, the "Law"
("*nomos*" in Greek for the Hebrew "*Torah*") metonymically standing in for

the whole of the relationship between God and man, as it does so often in Paul's Epistles (especially *Romans*) for the complex relationship between God and His Chosen People. Finally there is the sharp irony that the old Passover was a feast celebrating the escape from a king (pharaoh), while the new one offers a way to join the King of Kings at His table.

Given the Thomistic formulation of the Eucharist as "replacing and fulfilling" the rituals of the Old Covenant, it seems clear that this verse emphasizes the "replacement" part of the equation; "*terminat*" literally means "put an end to." And there is something like martial violence in the verbs of the last half: "*fugat*" ("puts to flight") and "*eliminat*" (literally, "throws out"; etymologically, "thrust out of the house or over the threshhold"). (Connelly's use of "displace" for both—indeed for all three phrases—strikes me as a little too pacific.)

In Aquinas's specific word order choices, more flexible in Latin than in English, he always makes the past precede the future, the old precede the new, so that the thing being replaced is followed by the thing replacing it. The English version makes "newness" or "the new" (*novitas*) put "oldness" or "the old" to flight, and "truth" (*veritas*) do the same to "shadows" (*umbras*)—the latter image being particularly apt as it is a common poetic trope to depict daylight as "chasing" night away. And by the parallelism of the three last lines, what is new and what is true is symbolized by "light" (*lux*) and what is old and obscure by "night" (*noctem*). This is not just an obvious reference to the traditional association of the Paschal mysteries with the rites of Spring and the return of light to the world (see the liturgy of the Easter Vigil). Here also, Aquinas is perhaps referencing John, the great evangelist of the Eucharist, and his initial formulation of Christ the Word as the "light" which the "darkness" could not "comprehend": *Et lux in tenebris lucet, et tenebrae eam non comprehenderunt* (Jn 1.5). I've always preferred to think of the "*non comprehenderunt*" not so much as being unable to "understand the light" as being unable to "smother the light"—in the sense of surround it, grasp it, keep it from illuminating.

Just a short note that elsewhere, I think, Thomas will not be so hard on the "shadows" that the truth "chases away." When he views them as "foreshadows," he will emphasize the "fulfillment" part of the "replacement and fulfillment" formulation. In that sense, there is surely a wonderfully deliberate ambiguity in the "dat panis caelicus figuris terminum" of the "Panis angelicus." A "termi-nus" is not simply an end—it is also a goal towards which one strives; so "the heavenly bread" gives the "prefigurings" both their "end" and their "fulfillment."

Verse Five

Quod in cœna Christus gessit,
Faciéndum hoc expréssit
  In sui memóriam.
Docti sacris institútis,
Panem, vinum, in salútis
  Consecrámus hóstiam.

What Christ at that supper did then
He ordered to be done again,
  In His sacred memory.
His holy orders we now obey,
We consecrate the host today—
  Bread and wine that sets us free.

Again, my translation is somewhat loose; and I use the English word "host"—which probably today evokes its sacramental meaning rather than its now archaic, but more accurate meaning of "victim." Connelly's prose version is:

> Christ wanted what he did at the supper to be repeated in his memory. And so we, in accordance with his holy directions, consecrate bread and wine to be salvation's Victim. (pp. 124, 126)

"Repeated" is Connelly's addition to the text, which merely says "this is to be done" (*faciendum hoc*). But my major quibble with Connelly's translation is with the word "wanted." I think the point of the verse is to clarify even more sharply that Christ *explicitly instituted* the Sacrament and *insisted* (imperative voice) that it continue to be performed after He was gone—*hoc facite in meam commemorationem* ("in my memory," or, "in memory of me") as only Luke (22.19) and Paul (1 Cor 11.24) record it. The word "*expressit*" means more than "a wanting" or "a desire"; it means "explicitly speaking." I also feel that "directions" for "*institutis*" is not quite as strong as it might be; the "institutes" of an organization are more like its formal charter, its

42

constitution and by-laws. Thomas's terminology is quite a bit more "legal-istic" than Connelly translates it. My literal translation would be:

> What Christ did at (that) meal, He expressly said was to be done in memory of him. Taught by His sacred instructions, we change bread and wine into the victim of (our) salvation.

It is perhaps worth noting that Aquinas's choice of words (*hoc, facere, in, sui, memoria*) follows roughly the Vulgate except in two instances: he uses the possessive pronoun instead of the possessive adjective ("*sui*" for "*suam*"); and he chooses "*memoria*" over the Vulgate's "*commemoratio*." Now the choice of "*sui*" is probably just to follow the rubric of the Roman Missal, which uses "*mei memoriam*"; and "*memoriam*" for "*commemora-tionem*" may also be for that reason, as well as for the sake of the prosody. But that choice may also have resulted in a lessening of what the Vulgate actually says. It is perhaps to put too fine a point on it, but Jerome chose "*commemoratio*" for his translation of the Greek "*anamnesis*"; and perhaps he chose it purposely to include the idea of a shared and celebrated memory "com-memoration," just as the Sacrament itself creates a shared union of the members with one another and with the Head—"com-munion." Just a thought, anyway. (The new Roman Missal, by the way, restored "*com-memorationem*.")

I also note that "*salus*" does not literally mean "salvation"; more accu-rately it means "health," "wholeness," or even "help"; and Thomas perhaps uses it as a synonym for "salvation" to mean all three—the "host" is the "help" which restores the soul to spiritual "health" and makes it "whole" again. At the same time, in a real sense, the three meanings of "*salus*" would apply equally well to bread and wine as purely physical nutrition. So the fifth line (*Panem, vinum in salutis*) can be read as primarily referring to *ma-terial* things, until they are elevated and transformed to *supernatural* realities by the "*Consecramus hostia*" of the next line—which in its sequential struc-ture captures precisely the chronology of consecration itself.

Moreover, there is a kind of oxymoronic flavor to the phrase "*salutis hos-tia*"; "to be saved" and "to be a victim" (and therefore *not* spared) are clearly opposites. (Thomas will visit this again in his great "*O salutaris hostia*.") The juxtaposition captures perfectly the theology of vicarious redemption that runs from the Old Covenant to the New: a victim is chosen to represent the people and their sins, and then that victim is sacrificed as expiation, and the people are, for the moment, spared. But in the Old Covenant, that sacrifice had to be offered anew, over and over again, because it was never perfect, while in the New it is made just once, because the sinless Christ is the "perfect victim"; the sin is once and for all expiated, and any further repetitions of the sacrificial act are not new sacrifices, but ritual commemorations of the one perfect sacrifice. This, at least, is the understanding of the author of the Epistle to the Hebrews (8.1–10.18).

So again, the point of the verse seems to be: this Sacrament is not something the Church *invented* to commemorate Christ's passion. We do it because Christ explicitly *instructed* us to do it. And somehow when we do it as He instructed us, we are not doing something different, but exactly the same thing He did. And what is new about it is: that it is a new *foundational* ritual, an institutional act at the center of a new Covenant.

*Interestingly, the old Roman Missal—before it was revised in 1969—suggested that Christ said two things which He is never recorded in scripture as having said, "mysterium fidei" (the mystery of faith) and "**aeterni** testamenti" (**eternal** testament), as well as something which only Paul records Him as saying: "Haec **quotiescumque** feceritis, in mei memoriam facietis" ("**Whenever** you do these (things), you should do (them) in memory of me") (MR, 1950, p. 391). Aquinas deals specifically with what constitutes the proper verbal form in ST 3.78.2 and 3; some of his arguments are quite fascinating, including the idea that the differences among the scriptural reports may have been because the early Christians wanted to keep the exact wording secret, as it was a "mysterium fidei."*

*In a further note, it is in "Hebrews" that the author of the Epistle uses the word "umbra" for the actions of the Israelite priests, **foreshadowing** in their imperfection the perfect sacrifice of Christ (Heb 10.1).*

Verse Six

Dogma datur Christiánis,
Quod in carnem transit panis,
  Et vinum in sánguinem.
Quod non capis, quod non vides,
Animósa firmat fides,
  Præter rerum ordinem.

This is part of our Christian creed:
That bread becomes His flesh indeed,
  And wine becomes His blood as well.
What you cannot see or perceive,
Fervent faith can help you believe,
  Far beyond what's natural.

This is perhaps the most specifically "theological" of the verses so far, right from the top with the technical term "*dogma*." So here it is: this is what must be believed, cannot be doubted (*non dubitur*). This is, literally, the dogma "given to Christians" (*datur Christianis*).

After the first three verses inviting the church to praise and identifying the specific object of that praise on this day (the Institution of Eucharist), with Verse Four Aquinas begins his exposition of exactly what that object entails. Verse Four identifies the particular "newness" (*novitas*) of the object, placing it at an inflection point between the old and the new, between shadow/night and truth/light. Verse Five further identifies it, not so much as a thing but as an event, an action, a thing done once and mandated to be done again, at Christ's insistence and in His memory.

Now with Verse Six we get, as it were, the doctrinal climax—what actually *is* done. And here, surprisingly, Connelly's translation becomes more of a paraphrase and a commentary, straying quite far from the actual Latin text:

> Christ's followers know by faith that bread is changed into his Flesh and wine into His blood. Man cannot understand this, cannot perceive it; but a lively faith affirms that the change,

which is outside the natural course of things, takes place. (p. 126)

A literal translation is quite different:

> (This) dogma is given to Christians: that bread changes into flesh, and wine into blood. What you can't grasp, what you can't see, a strong faith confirms, outside the order of things. (*My translation.*)

First of all, by retaining the singular personal pronoun "you," Thomas identifies the intended recipient of his teaching, the listener, to whom he is passing on what he has thought about (*contemplata aliis tradere*). *You* can't see it, *you* can't understand it, not according to the natural order of things, so you must accept it on faith as true. (The "you" is, of course, inclusive of Thomas himself, who—like any other Christian—is unable to grasp or see the change.)

Then there is a nice parallelism between the last three lines of the previous verse and the first three lines of this one. The *"Docti"* ("taught") of the previous verse and the *"Dogma"* ("doctrine," that which is taught) of this verse establish a echoing similarity, while the first person plural of the previous verse (*consecramus* the first "we" in the sequence) and the second person singular of this verse (*capis, vides*) establish a subtle difference. This, as we shall see, marks the difference between the body of the faithful (including priests) who must *believe* in the transformation, and the subset of the ordained members who, on Christ's instructions, are obligated and empowered to *effect* the transformation. This is not a separation that Aquinas explores further in this sequence, perhaps because he rightly wants to keep the focus on Christ (the Host of the Feast) and on His "dinner guests"; but it is one he insists on in his *Summa* (*ST* 3.82.1).

The last two lines of this verse re-affirm the truth of the transformation, even though it is imperceptible to mortal eyes or understanding. *Faith alone* is the firm foundation of that truth (*ST* 3.75.1). This statement in a slightly different form will recur in the *Tantum Ergo*: *"Praestet fides supplementum / Sensuum defecti"* (literally, let faith offer a reinforcement to the defect of the senses; more colloquially, let faith fill in the gap where the senses fall short).

But of particular importance, I think, is Aquinas's use of the phrase *"transit in"* (literally, "to go over into"). In the *Summa*, Aquinas spends an astonishing amount of time trying to analyze exactly the nature of this "transition," even as he admits it is "outside the nature of things." He does so because as a confirmed disciple of Aristotle (whose physics and metaphysics he generally accepted as true) as well as a confirmed follower of Christ, he would prefer that it might be understood in a way that is not *repugnant* to natural understanding, even though it may be *beyond* it. So, for example, he insists that Christ's flesh may be said to be made "out of bread" (*ex pane*) but not "of bread" (*de pane*) (*ST* 3.75.8); that the change is instantaneous and not gradual (*ST* 3.75.7); and that it is a true "change" from one thing into another, and not the annihilation of one thing to make room for another (*ST* 3.75.3).

The importance of all this for me is not so much in the granular details, but in the admirable relentlessness of Thomas's intellect, his insistence on squaring even the most intricate and complex mysteries of dogma with what he believed to be true about the natural world. It is a complement to his aggressive "realism" and his confidence in the truth of both reason and revelation that he dared to chase those two (for him) ultimately reconcilable truths so deeply into the most challenging corners of his faith. *Fides quaerens intellectum* (faith seeking understanding) is what it used to be called.

I always wonder how Thomas would respond today to scientific discoveries that seem to be in conflict with long-standing Church doctrine. Would he still insist there was only "one truth," or would he yield to the now fashionable position that the "truths" of religion and the "truths" of science are separate kinds of truth? I suspect he would still strive mightily to reconcile them, as the Church has occasionally done, though her record is hardly stellar in that regard. But she's a huge craft, this barque of Peter, and turns on a troubled sea are always painfully slow.

Verse Seven (Part One)

Sub divérsis speciébus,
Signis tantum, et non rebus,
  Latent res exímiæ.
Caro cibus, sanguis potus:
Manet tamen Christus totus,
  Sub utráque spécie.

Underneath two different figurings—
Only signs, and not really things,
  Lie unique realities.
His blood to drink, His flesh to eat;
Yet is Christ the Lord complete,
  Under either shape one sees.

In this verse Aquinas continues his use of somewhat technical theological language with the Latin words *"species," "signum,"* and *"res."* In the introduction, I presented—in advance of our analysis of the poetry of the sequence—one of his most crucial formulations: that Sacraments are composed of both signs and the realities which those signs represent. In the *Summa,* his word for a "sacramental sign" is simply *"sacramentum"*; his word for the reality it represents is *"res"*—which basically means "thing." But the relationship in the Eucharist is more complex than that; there are a couple of levels. This verse deals with the *first* level: between the physical sign (here the appearance—*species*—of bread and wine) and the first level of reality—*res*—the real presence of Christ's Body and Blood. At the next deeper level, that Body and Blood together, besides being a reality, is itself a further sacred sign of the Mystical Body, composed of Christ and all the saved in union with him and one another.

In the *Summa,* *"species"* ("outward appearance") is Thomas's chosen word to describe all that remains of the bread and wine after the Consecration, what Aquinas defines in more philosophical language as their "accidents." And it is with some relief, I think, that we find Thomas avoiding that more abstract and metaphysical level of language. Nowhere in the sequence do we find the unmistakable Aristotelianisms of *substantia, accidens, forma,* or *materia.* Nor does the crucial coinage "*transubstantio*" appear, despite its importance in his theology and in the Church's definitions. His vocabulary in the *Lauda Sion* is as much as possible drawn from familiar sources rather than erudite ones. In fact, one of the wonders of his poetry is that he can be so precise, so compressed, so dense in his hymns of praise to the Eucharist *without* resorting to the complex terminology that was necessary to instruct students of theology. And to do it in neatly rhyming tetrameters!

At the same time, Thomas never loses sight of his other crucial formulation: Christ's Flesh and Blood are really present at that first level of signification as food and drink (*Caro cibus, sanguis potus*). It's like a reminder: every time we may be tempted by the awesome realities (*res eximiae*) of the Sacrament to withdraw in humble adoration, Aquinas pulls us back into an immediacy with the Sacrament by identifying it as nourishment to be consumed. That tension between those two elements of the Sacrament, one that tends to distance it from us (as the divine is distanced from the human) and the other that draws us into an intimate relationship with it (as our food and drink) mirrors the same tension that exists in the other saving event, without which the Eucharist would not be possible, the Divine Word's assumption of a mortal body in the mystery of the Incarnation. Truly God and truly man.

In the last two lines of the verse, while still continuing to explore with theological exactitude the doctrinal aspects of the Eucharist, Aquinas also begins a move into more pastoral concerns. In a sense, one might say this verse is concerned with resolving the "dualities" of the Sacrament, both theologically and practically. There is the "horizontal" duality of two *species* (the appearance of *both* bread and wine) and two *res* (the separate Body and Blood). Then there is the "vertical" duality of the relationship of "signs" to the "things signified." This vertical duality is resolved by Thomas's explanation of sacred signification and the relationship between appearance and realities. But in a real, pastoral sense, the horizontal duality presents a possible problem. Just how separate are the Flesh and Blood?

The reason there may be a pastoral problem is that apparently Jesus made it quite clear that: "Very truly, I tell you, unless you eat the flesh of the Son of Man and drink his blood, you have no life in you" (John 6:54).

Yet for centuries the Sacrament was administered to the faithful under one *species* only, that of bread. How to square the *praxis* with the *dogma*? Aquinas's answer is that the whole Christ (*Christus totus*) remains (*manet*) under *either* appearance (*sub utraque specie*)—or, perhaps better, Christ remains whole under either appearance. (The Latin syntax permits either—*utraque*—reading, and in a sense *both* readings, which, of course, makes the poetry even denser and richer.)

His is a complex solution, with many surprises in it; so I'm going to stop here and finish our examination of Verse Seven in second part.

Verse Seven (Part Two)

Manet tamen Christus totus,
  Sub utráque spécie.

Yet is Christ the Lord complete,
  Under either shape one sees.

Aquinas deals with the issue of *how* Christ is in the Eucharist primarily in Question 76. We focus here on the last two lines, where syntactically, the singulars (*Christus, totus, specie, manet*) contrast with the plurals of the first three lines (*speciebus, signis, rebus, res eximiae, latent*).

As I suggested earlier, this is not just a doctrinal question, but also a pastoral one; and Thomas seems to be moving with this verse, and the next, into the area not just of the *nature* of the Sacrament, but its *reception*: how those who receive the Sacrament are to understand what they are receiving. Communicants under *one* species—only the bread, for example—may wonder if they are fulfilling Christ's command and receiving the "whole Christ" (*Christus totus*), Body and Blood. And even under *both* species, they may well wonder if they are receiving not just His Body and Blood, but His soul and divinity as well.

Aquinas's answer to the second question is that "*totus Christus*" necessarily includes His soul and divinity (*ST* 3.76.1); the bread and wine are changed into His Body and Blood by the "power" of the Sacrament; but by the fact that Christ's body, once assumed, was never "set aside" by the Godhead, it follows that "wherever the body of Christ is, there, of necessity, must the Godhead be." He calls this necessary linkage "real concomitance" (*naturalis concomitancia*).

I'm not sure this a particularly persuasive argument; actually I wouldn't call it a proof at all, but more of an attempt to understand what his faith tells him must be true. But that same drive to take reason as far as it can go in grasping mysteries like this one, also leads him to reach a truly astonishing conclusion in a subsequent hypothetical: "had this sacrament been celebrated during those three days when He was dead, the soul of Christ would not have been there." A truly breath-taking conclusion!

But once Aquinas has insisted that Christ truly died on the cross as a matter of faith, and once he has defined death as the separation of the soul from the body, then he has no choice but to reach this conclusion; not to do so would require either denying the actuality of Christ's death or the definition of death itself, thus undermining an essential element of his philosophy. This need to assert both truths forces the conclusion—because the Sacrament is not a symbol, but the real presence of Christ *as He is at the present moment of consecration*. For the Sacrament after the Resurrection to be the glorified body of Christ, and therefore the sacred sign of the Mystical Body of Christ, Aquinas must allow for the "three days" when Christ, as man, was neither alive nor yet glorified. This pursuit of an understanding that seems to lead to near absurdities may strike some as a form of intellectual hubris; but to me, it is a mark of Aquinas's realism, his belief that natural and supernatural truths can be reconciled, and his astonishing and consistent—and humble—willingness to follow the truth wherever it leads him.

As to the first issue—whether reception under a single species is sufficient—Aquinas answers in the second article that, yes, the whole Christ is present under each species (*ST* 3.76.2), with pretty much the same argument from "real concomitance" and even the same hypothetical. As His body and blood are one *now*—i.e., post Resurrection—then they are equally united in the Sacrament *celebrated now*. But were the same Sacrament celebrated during the "three days" when He was in the tomb, then "the body of Christ would have been under the species of the bread, but without the blood; and, under the species of the wine, the blood would have been present without the body, as it was then, in fact."

I love that final phrase, "in fact"—in Latin, "in rei veritate," in the truth of the thing. For Thomas, truth is not some distant, floating cloud requiring only a hazy and tepid agreement; truth is real, truth is interconnected, truth has consequences.

Verse Eight

A suménte non concísus,
Non confráctus, non divísus:
  Integer accípitur.
Sumit unus, sumunt mille:
Quantum isti, tantum ille:
  Nec sumptus consúmitur.

He gives Himself for our nourishment,
Not divided, broken, or rent,
  He is consumed whole, complete.
Each one receives as much as all,
Christ is inexhaustible,
  Whether one or thousands eat.

This is perhaps my favorite verse in the *Lauda Sion*. I particularly love the soaring melody of its traditional setting in Gregorian chant. So it irks me that I have not been able to translate it at a level of accuracy, economy, and compression—of sheer beauty—that it deserves. Connelly's prose translation is fairly accurate as to meaning:

> The communicant receives the complete Christ—uncut, unbroken, undivided. Whether one receive or a thousand, the one receives as much as the thousand. Nor is Christ diminished by being received. (p. 126)

But it takes him thirty words to do what Aquinas manages in twenty-one. And not just the end rhymes, but the internal rhymes and assonances are lost in the prose (*tantum, quantum*; *non, non, non, nec*; the four repetitions of *sum-*). Connelly's grammatically correct but awkward subjunctive in the second half ("whether one receive") and the resulting syntactical subordination of one clause to another (in my verse translation as well) both weaken the forthrightness of Aquinas's lapidary and insistent present indicative clauses:

> One eats, thousands eat:
> They (eat) as much as he:
> Nor is the eaten, eaten up.
>   (*My translation*)

And notice as well the piquancy of having the "dividing words" (*concisus, confractus, divisus*) not only *precede* the unifying word (*integer*), but also *divide* the recipient from the thing received—Christ—who is not even named in the entire verse.

> By the eater—not cut,
> Not broken, not divided—
> Whole is (He) received.
>   (*My translation*)

Another striking chiasmic construction, another win for Latin, another lesson in humility for the translator.

As for the *Summa*, Thomas deals with this issue in Article Three of Question 76: "Whether Christ is entire under every part of the species of the bread and wine?" After listing the typical objections, Aquinas cites Augustine in support:

> Each receives Christ the Lord, Who is entire under every morsel, nor is He less in each portion, but bestows Himself entire under each. (*ST* 3.76.3)

His further reasoning is quite complex, drawn from previous distinctions he has made between substance and accident, and between nature, locality, and dimensionality; but happily, these deeper philosophical arguments nowhere surface in the language of the sequence, where Aquinas is content to *assert* the truths in the most striking language possible rather than *prove* them in the most obscure—as is totally appropriate in hymns of praise.

That his intentions here are primarily pastoral is made clear by his return to direct address to the listener ("don't hesitate, remember") in Verse Ten, a verse which directly continues the thinking of Verse Eight, after a digression onto another subject in Verse Nine (which also has a form of direct address). But more about that in the next session.

I suspect that the cause of this "digression" is more poetic than thematic, as it allows Aquinas to continue in Verse Nine, the linguistic concentration and parallelism of Verse Eight, before the shift in prosodic structure in Verse Ten to the more expansive form of two four-line stanzas.

Verse Nine

Sumunt boni, sumunt mali:
Sorte tamen inæquáli,
  Vitæ vel intéritus.
Mors est malis, vita bonis:
Vide paris sumptiónis
  Quam sit dispar éxitus.

Good and bad alike may receive,
The good will joy, the bad will grieve,
  So unlike, the fates they meet.
Life to the good, but death to the bad,
See what diverse ends may be had
  From the same food that they eat.

This verse, like the previous one, is still about the reception of the Sacrament and its effect upon the receiver. Aquinas deals with these issues primarily in Questions 79 and 80. I look at this particular verse as a kind of digression, because the concerns of Verse Eight flow more naturally into the concerns of Verse Ten: essentially confirming the *oneness* of the Sacrament when there is clear *duality* in its species (bread and wine), and potential *multiplicity* in its reception (both in the breaking of the host and the distribution of multiple (and possibly fragmented) hosts to the faithful.

Verse Nine deals with neither of those issues, but rather focuses upon the effect the Sacrament has upon different communicants. Aquinas's critical scriptural text on this primary issue is from Paul: "He that eateth and drinketh unworthily, eateth and drinketh judgment to himself" (1 Cor 11:29); and the articles in which he deals with it are Four and Five of Question 80 (*ST* 3.80.4–5).

As I said earlier, Aquinas continues the prosodic techniques of parallelism, contrast, terseness, and compression that he used to such advantage in Verse Eight—and that tax the translator. The literal translation would display that economy:

The good eat, the bad eat,
But (with) the unequal lot (*sorte*, fate)
Of life or ruination (*interitus*, ruin).
The bad (get) death, the good, life:
Look, from similar eating,
How different may be the outcome (*exitus*).
(*My prose translation*)

One might well construe this as a pastoral warning to the faithful to avoid approaching the Sacrament unworthily. The "look" (*vide*) in the fifth line is probably a relic of an imperative verb whose frequent use has reduced it to no more than something like "O"—as in "O, how different"—but the unexpressed "you" is still lurking underneath the idiom. And in the move to the next verse, the "you" of the listener becomes expressed rather than "understood."

Fascinatingly, it is in the second layer of signification of the Sacrament—where Christ's Body and Blood are themselves the deeper sacred sign of the Mystical Body—that Aquinas grounds his primary objection to the unworthy reception of the Sacrament:

> whoever receives this sacrament, expresses thereby that he is made one with Christ, and incorporated in His members; and this is done by living faith, which no one has who is in mortal sin. And therefore it is manifest that whoever receives this sacrament while in mortal sin, is guilty of *lying to this sacrament*, and consequently of sacrilege, because he profanes the sacrament: and therefore he sins mortally. (*ST* 3.80.4; emphasis mine)

One might have expected profaneness in receiving Christ's real Body and Blood would have been the primary fault, but surprisingly Thomas finds it in *lying* about one's membership in the Mystical Body. That's where the true "sacrilege" is, the true profanity—in the false claim of communion, not in the touching of the sacred body. After all, says Thomas, Christ, in "His proper species" allowed Himself to be touched by sinners, but they "did not incur the sin of lying to Godlike things, as sinners do in receiving this sacrament." And Aquinas *was* a stickler about "lying"—it was for him, who so valued the integral connection between the mind and the word, an intrinsic evil (*ST* 2-2.110).

There are quite a few more subtle and not so subtle refinements in the *Summa* on the possible state of mind of a "sinner" approaching the Sacrament, including whether willful ignorance of sin or partial contrition for it may be mitigating factors. There is even a question of whether "nocturnal pollution" is sinful enough to exclude one from the Sacrament (it depends). It is also in this question, as we noted before, that Aquinas raises the issue of the priest's right or duty to deny the Sacrament to one whom He knows to be a sinner (again, it depends). We should be grateful none of these concerns are raised in the sequence.

This is the penultimate verse in the main body of the sequence. Verse Ten, which we shall consider next, finishes off (demum, "last of all") the pastoral section. Then Verse Eleven—the "Ecce Panis Angelorum"—presents a kind of doctrinal summary, repositioning the Sacrament in the past, present, and future; followed by Verse Twelve, a prayer made directly to Jesus to include mortal men in His Mystical Body by "feeding" them.

Verse Ten

Fracto demum Sacraménto,
Ne vacílles, sed memento,
Tantum esse sub fragménto,
  Quantum toto tégitur.
Nulla rei fit scissúra:
Signi tantum fit fractúra:
Qua nec status nec statúra
  Signáti minúitur.

After all the breaking is done,
Each part holds as much as one;
This remember and do not shun
  A sliver of the Sacrament.
No reality is broken,
What is split is just a token,
But the thing which is bespoken
  Suffers no diminishment.

This verse speaks directly to the communicants of the Sacrament, who may be harboring concerns about exactly what happens in the "Breaking of the Bread." Is Christ broken? Am I receiving only a piece of Him if I receive a "fragment?"

In the *Summa*, Thomas answers these doubts directly in Question 76, Article 3, as noted before in the section on Verse Eight:

> And therefore it is manifest that the entire Christ is under every part of the species of the bread, even while the host remains entire, and not merely when it is broken. (*ST* 3.76.3)

He does so again—somewhat obliquely—in Question 77, Article 7: "Whether the sacramental species are broken in this sacrament?" There he re-asserts that it is only the species and not the body of Christ which is broken—

> First of all, because it [the Risen Christ's glorified Body] is incorruptible and impassible: secondly, because it is entire under every part, as was shown above . . . which is contrary to the nature of a thing broken. (*ST* 3.77.7)

His return in the sequence to this question—which he had already dealt with two verses earlier—may suggest that it was an important pastoral concern for him; and his much more personal tone here—"remember" (*memento*), "you shouldn't hesitate" (*ne vacilles*, literally "don't waver")—reveals a more intimate, encouraging voice.

There are some other important word choices in the Latin that are worth a closer look. The "*demum*" ("finally") in the first line may mean either of two things, I think. It may be a simple marker indicting that this verse is the last of the "instructional" verses of the sequence, which began in Verse Four, with Verses One through Three having served as the introductory invitation to praise. This is how Connelly views it and translates it. But it is possible that it means something like "once the Sacrament is finally broken" or "even after the Sacrament is broken" (*Fracto demum Sacramento*). This meaning harks back to the passage in Question 76: that Christ remains whole in "each part of the species of the bread" both *before* and *after* it is broken. This is in fact the meaning I have taken in my verse translation.

The "*tegitur*" in line four actually means "is covered"; so the literal translation would be: "remember / There is as much under the fragment / As is covered by the whole." Also, in lines five and six, Thomas returns to his dependable verbal distinction between sign and reality (*signum* and *res*); and interestingly he uses subjunctive verbs in those same lines to add a dash of necessity—literally, "There would not be a dividing of the reality, / There would be only breaking of the sign." And for the word "only," Aquinas reuses the "*tantum*" from line three, where it meant "so much" or "as much" and was more of a conjunction than an adverb. This is a typical rhetorical figure of speech (another of Shakespeare's favorites), repeating a word used earlier to mean something different ("antanaclasis," for those who care about such things).

Finally, the last line of my translation seriously compresses the last two lines of Thomas's verse, which contain the cognate, alliterating, and almost untranslatable *"nec status nec statura."* Whatever they are, neither of them, the sequence, says "is diminished" (*minuitur*). Connelly translates them as "condition or size"; transliterally, they might be "state or stature." Perhaps the closest we can come in paraphrase is "essence or extent," with "extent" (or literally "height") being a poetic "stand-in" for "integrity" or "wholeness." (Both words are derived from the Latin *"stare,"* to stand—as is Aquinas's favorite word for the non-visible reality of the Sacrament, its "substance,"—the Body of Christ.)

I admit my poetic version is closer to a paraphrase than an accurate translation, but the addition of two more rhyming lines creates a real challenge for rhyme-poor English. And of course inflectionally rich Latin provides far more opportunities for creative word order than is possible in English, which depends so much on word position to establish syntax.

Verse Eleven, Part One

Ecce panis Angelórum,
Factus cibus viatórum:
Vere panis filiórum,
  Non mitténdus cánibus.
In figúris præsignátur,
Cum Isaac immolátur:
Agnus paschæ deputátur
  Datur manna pátribus.

This is truly Angels's bread,
Giv'n to earthly pilgrims instead;
On such bread are children fed,
  It is not cast away on curs.
It is prefigured by the ram,
That spares the son of Abraham,
By the slaughter of the Paschal lamb,
  By manna giv'n our forefathers.

This eleventh verse is, at one and the same time, a recapitulation of the dominant "food" theme, a positioning of the Eucharist in the past, present, and future, and the most scriptural of all the verses in the Sequence, highlighting the "replacement/fulfillment" theme. Rhetorically, it stands as the song's "conclusion"—the first three verses being the "introduction," and the next seven being the "body" of the argument, with the twelfth and final verse being the "coda,"—namely, a prayer addressed to Jesus, while all the verses before were addressed to the Church (*Zion*).

As Connelly points out in his note to the *Panis Angelicus*, the "bread of angels" trope is borrowed from the Old Testament, specifically from Psalm 77 and Wisdom 16 (Connelly, p. 123):

The bread of heaven he gave them; man ate the bread of angels.
(Ps 77:24–25; *my translation*)
You nourished your people with the bread of angels, and gave them bread from heaven prepared without labor, having in it

all deliciousness and the sweetness of every taste. (Wis 16:20; *my translation*)

Both these, of course, refer to the miracle of the manna in the desert, and both appear in scriptural passages recapitulating the history of the Israelites in an effort to remind them of all the favors God has showered upon His Chosen People. But the deeper point which both passages make, and which Aquinas capitalizes on, is that this nourishment is, as the Jerusalem Bible translates it, "the bread of Immortals." It is properly—albeit metaphorically—the nourishment of those enjoying eternal happiness in heaven; and yet, miraculously, it is given to those *not living* in heavenly bliss, but *journeying* towards it. It is "made the food of travelers" (*factus cibus viatorum*). It is both an aid on the journey and a foretaste of the journey's end.

These two lines locate the Eucharist simultaneously in three timeframes: in the past history of the Old Covenant, specifically the miracle of the manna, which is a "figure" of it; in the present moment of the mortal journey, for which the Eucharist is the food taken and eaten on the way (*viaticum*); and in the future bliss of the union of all creation—including the angels—under Christ in eternal glory. Thus, says Thomas elsewhere, "*viaticum*" is a perfectly appropriate name for the Sacrament—though "it does not at once admit us to glory, but bestows on us the power of coming unto glory" (*ST* 3.79.2).

The next two lines bring us firmly into the New Testament, referencing Jesus's encounter with the Canaanite woman, who was persistent in begging the man she initially called "Son of David" to heal her daughter of an evil spirit. In Mark's version (Mk 7:24–30) she is explicitly identified as a Gentile.

> He said in answer, "It is not fair to take the children's bread and to cast it to the dogs." But she said, "Yes, Lord; for even the dogs eat of the crumbs that fall from their masters' table." Then Jesus answered, "O woman, great is thy faith! Let it be done to thee as thou wilt." And her daughter was healed from that moment. (Mt 15:26–28)

I have always found this encounter fascinating; it is only one of two in which Jesus praises the faith of a contemporary non-Jew—the Centurion with the sick servant/son is the other (Mt 8:5–13 and Lk 7:1–10). But what I find particularly striking is how unpredictable and surprising Jesus's encounters sometimes can be.

Here, rather startlingly, He responds to the desperate woman initially with an insult, calling her a dog. Though there is good evidence in the Greek that He softened the insult somewhat by His word choice—which other translations render as "house dogs" or "family dogs"; still "dog" it is. (My ".curs" is, therefore, probably too strong, but I needed the rhyme.) And the woman, with a marvelous *"contorquatio argumenti"*—"twisting the argument" back in her favor by using her opponent's own words—gains both the miracle and Christ's praise for the depth of her faith.

But how exactly—beyond offering another possible New Testament "prefiguring" like the multiplication of the loaves and fishes—does it fit here in the sequence? First, it emphasizes the absolute necessity for faith in the Sacrament in order to receive the healing graces of the Sacrament—a critical point in Aquinas's exposition of the doctrine: "this sacrifice, which is the memorial of our Lord's Passion, has no effect except in those who are united with this sacrament through faith and charity" (*ST* 3.79.7). Second, therefore, it is a Sacrament available, it would seem, only to the members of the Church, those who believe in it, not to outsiders any more than to animals.

But third, there is the astonishing *counter-movement* in referencing this incident of the Canaanite woman. After all, Jesus did grant her wish because of her *faith,* even though that faith was in Him personally and not the professed faith of the Israelite community. And in the parallel story of the Centurion, Jesus goes on to praise his similar faith as greater than what He has found in Israel, and then uses the image of a *feast* to suggest a much more universal effect:

> And I tell you that many will come from the east and from the west, and will feast with Abraham and Isaac and Jacob in the kingdom of heaven, but the children of the kingdom will be put forth into the darkness outside. (Mt 8:11–12)

So perhaps we should not be too swift to see these two lines as emphasizing the *exclusionary* nature of the Sacrament, and relish the power of its *inclusionary* promise. There is a real sense in which the Sacrament *creates* the larger community of believers, rather than *being limited* to it, bestows on all of us "the power of coming unto glory." And in that sense it is the bread of "the children" who make up the larger family of man, and not just of the more immediate family of Church members. Such saving "faith" is perhaps not best defined as "belief in the truth of a dogma," but better as faith in Him who is "the Way, the Truth, and the Life."

The second half of this verse, dealing with more Old Testament prefigurings, I will explore in the next section.

Verse Eleven, Part Two

In figúris præsignátur,
Cum Isaac immolátur:
Agnus paschæ deputátur
 Datur manna pátribus.

It is prefigured by the ram,
That spares the son of Abraham,
By the slaughter of the Paschal lamb,
 By manna giv'n our forefathers.

The last half of Verse Eleven specifically revisits the Old Testament prefigurings of the Eucharist. Aquinas here names three: Isaac, the Paschal Lamb, and manna. I confess great discomfort at replacing in my translation Isaac with the ram—the victim that God provided in his place (*Deus providebit sibi victimam*)—but there was that pesky rhyme; and in my own defense, I reply (*respondeo*) that after all it is the ram (*aries*) and not Isaac that is immolated (*immolatur*) (Gen 22.1–14).

Aquinas deals with Eucharistic prefigurings in Question 73, Article 6: "Whether the Paschal Lamb was the chief figure of this sacrament?" He answers that question, of course, with a distinction, a familiar one—the three levels of signification. At the first level, that of the sign alone (bread and wine), perhaps another figure—like that of Melchisedech's offering of bread and wine—might be the preferred sign. But the Paschal Lamb "foreshadowed this sacrament" *at all three levels.* Because it was eaten with unleavened loaves, it prefigures the first level. Because it was eaten at Passover when Christ died, it prefigures the saving Passion of Christ (the Lamb of God) and His Glorified Body, which is both sign and reality. And because the blood of the Paschal Lamb preserved and freed the people of Israel, it prefigures the deepest effect and deepest reality of the Sacrament, eventual salvation—which Thomas elsewhere identifies as full incorporation into the Mystical Body of Christ.

Oddly, in this article there are no responses to the earlier objections—one of them suggesting that manna might be a better prefiguring. Thomas merely states that there is no need to answer those objections because, after he has made his central point, "the answer to the Objections is manifest." But it is clear from the sequence that he thought manna was a prefiguring—just not the best. And the same goes for Isaac, though he never mentions him in his Eucharistic Questions in the *Summa*.

I find it fascinating that Aquinas uses all present tenses in these lines, which I have tried to honor somewhat, even in my mistranslation ("that *spares* the son of Abraham"). It is almost as if, in their act of prefiguring, they are present again in the sacred Sacrament they prefigure. Thus "the heavenly bread gives them their end," as the *Panis Angelicus* says (*Dat panis caelicus figuris terminum*), but it also gives them the goal (*terminus*) to which they were—are—pointing: replacement *and* fulfillment.

It is also noteworthy that in Thomas's Latin, the Paschal Lamb is not "slaughtered" but "appointed for the Pasch," as Connelly translates it. In my translation I have switched the predicates between the ram and the lamb, by having the ram be the "stand-in" or "deputy" (*deputatur*) for Isaac, and having the lamb actually "sacrificed" (*immolatur*). Both, by the way, offer a prefiguring of the theme of "vicarious redemption," which the third Old Testament figure—the manna—does not. Yet neatly, the verse closes where it began, with the manna, and with our "forefathers" (*patribus*), of whom we are the spiritual descendants; so they too are part of the family.

Whether our spiritual "forefathers"—the patriarchs—were also saved by Christ's Passion, and presumably by its commemoration in the Eucharist, is something Thomas explores in ST 3.52.5. The image of Gentiles coming from the east and west to "feast with Abraham, Isaac, and Jacob in the kingdom of heaven" (Mt 8:11) would suggest so.

And while we are on the subject of Eucharistic symbolism, or more accurately on the relationship of the sacramental sign (sacramentum) to the sacramental reality (res), I think it is worth remembering what excellent signs bread and wine are. Of course "food" is the most important signification—the appearance of material nourishment for the reality of spiritual nourishment. But it goes much deeper than that, I think. There is the fact of two different species rather than one: the separation of the bread and wine is the sacramental image of the real separation of body and blood in death and thus of Christ's sacrifice. Add to that, both species are already the result of "substantial" transformations—the bread by baking and the wine by fermentation.

And then we can go even deeper—and these next thoughts are mine rather than Thomas's. Bread and wine do not occur naturally; they are, quite literally, the product of "culture"—they are social artifacts; they are made by processes learned and passed down through generations. Therefore they already include the idea of a shared community in their creation. Next, they are not simple foods. Grapes must be pressed, wheat must be ground and winnowed; so there is already a symbolism of one kind of destruction leading to a higher kind of perfection. Next, they are wholes made of parts: many grapes go to the making of a single wine, many grains of wheat to the making of a single loaf; therefore they are good images of the many being combined into the one. Next, in almost all cultures, breaking bread with others and sharing a cup with them are symbols of peace and harmony, of social "communion." And in order to share, bread must be "broken" and wine, "poured out." At almost all levels of signification, bread and wine seem to be ideal sacramental signs.

Verse Twelve

Bone pastor, panis vere,
Jesu, nostri miserére:
Tu nos pasce, nos tuére:
Tu nos bona fac vidére
    In terra vivéntium.
Tu, qui cuncta scis et vales:
Qui nos pascis hic mortáles:
Tuos ibi commensáles,
Cohærédes et sodáles,
    Fac sanctórum cívium.

Loving Shepherd, O Lord Jesus,
Living Bread, have mercy on us,
Lead us, feed us, Lord, and bring us,
To see all things glorious,
    In the land of the living.
You that know and ground the universe,
Feeder here of mortal travelers,
Make us there your table-sharers,
Comrades and co-inheritors
    With the saints in heaven.

The sequence draws to an end, appropriately enough, with a prayer. Actually, a double prayer. The long ten-line verse is composed of two five-line stanzas, each making roughly the same appeal: "Lord, you who feed us now, bring us to heaven." The repetition is perhaps a response to Christ's insistence that when we pray we should be persistent. When the Apostles beg Him to teach them how to pray, He responds with the "Our Father" (Lk 11:1–5). But He does not stop there; He goes on to tell them of the importunate "friend" who keeps bothering the householder at night for a few loaves of bread to feed his unexpected guests:

I say to you, although he will not get up and give to him because he is his friend, but because of his persistence he will get up and give him all he needs. (Lk 11:8)

So perhaps by doubling the plea, Aquinas provides a model of such persistence. And if we are to give any credence to Martin Luther's "Whoever sings, prays twice" (*bis cantat qui orat*), by including these prayers in a sequence, Aquinas "quadruples" their effectiveness.

However, it is worth noting that they are not simple repetitions; there is both a sameness and a difference. Both, after the strong evocations of the biblical past in the previous verse, are strongly rooted in the present and the future. Each, at the beginning of its stanza, asks for nourishment in this life—a life which the first implies is pitiable and dangerous and the second categorizes as "mortal." And both, at the end, look forward to the eternal happiness of heaven.

The nuanced difference between them is that the *first* stanza, in spite of the plural "us" (*nos, nostri*), seems to emphasize the future personal salvation of the individual in the Beatific Vision—"make us see all good things" (*Tu nos bona fac videre*)—in "the land of the living" (*in terra viventium*). The *second*, however, seems to stress the communal universality of that salvation. Christ is now not named as the Good Shepherd who is called to "feed and look after us" (*Tu nos pasce, nos tuere*), but as one who "knows and strengthens—or validates—*everything*" (*Tu qui cuncta scis et vales*). The nourishment asked for "here" (*hic*) is for the human race (*mortales*); and the future happiness "there" (*ibi*) is to be "your table-partners" (*tuos commensales*), and "the co-heirs and companions of the sainted citizens" (*Cohaeredes et sodales . . . sanctorum civium*).

Thus, the first stanza seems to emphasize the Eucharistic effect (*effectum*) of saving grace and "fitness to glory" (*adeptio gloriae*)—"glory" meaning the eternal happiness of heaven (*ST* 3.79.1 and 2). But the second stanza specifically references the "communion of saints" (*communio sanctorum*), which Thomas clearly identifies as the Mystical Body and the deepest reality (*res*) of the Sacrament. And he cites Augustine to the effect that nothing can slake man's spiritual hunger and thirst, except for the Eucharistic food and drink, "which maketh them who partake thereof to be immortal and incorruptible, *in the fellowship of the saints*" (*ST* 3.79.2, emphasis my own).

I'm not sure Connelly gets it quite right when he links *commensales* and *cohearedes* together ("Your guests in heaven and co-heirs with you," and then links only *sodales* with the saints ("And companions of heaven's citizens") (p. 128). But he is certainly correct in his summary of the final verse: "A prayer that all who share this table here below may be gathered at the heavenly feast and table" (p. 129).

All that remains is a summary of our explorations, to be made in the next section "Amen. Alleluia."

Amen. Alleluia

So what, in sum, have we discovered about Aquinas's *Lauda Sion*?

Rhetorically, it is deftly organized. There are twelve verses in all.

Three introductory verses call us to praise in song, identify the topic of the praise (the Eucharist), and describe the manner of the praise (full, loud, beautiful, joyous, and soulful) and the occasion of the praise (the feast of Corpus Christi, honoring the institution of the Sacrament).

Eight verses make up the body of the sequence, each one exploring a single element of the Eucharist in more detail, just as Aquinas does in the Questions and Articles of his *Summa Theologiae*. But here the exploration is not so much theological as celebratory and pastoral; the verses prove nothing, analyze with only a light touch; mostly, they assert and clarify without too much explicitly theological jargon. It is not so much a mental exercise as a mental exultation—a *mentis jubilatio*. In that way, the sequence shows itself a true extension of an Alleluia, which is originally what all sequences were.

The twelfth and final verse concludes with a double prayer, linking the reception of the Sacrament with the promise of glory at the heavenly feast.

Doctrinally, Aquinas maintains throughout his three crucial insights in the Sacrament: that it is essentially **food**; that the level of "**signification**" **is three-fold** (the appearances of bread and wine, the Real Presence of the Body of Christ, and the Mystical Body of all believers united under the Head); and that the Sacrament is a **fulfillment and replacement** of foreshadowing rites and events in the Old Testament, even as the New Covenant is a fulfillment and replacement of the Old. These insights further allow him to locate the Sacrament in three "time zones," as it were: the **past** (both the actual time of its Institution and the Passion as well as the foreshadowing events in the more distant history of the Chosen People); the **present** (whenever the Sacrament is celebrated today and we partake of it, receiving not only Christ's Body and Blood but also the concomitant "character" and grace that fit us for heaven); and the **future**, (when, in communion with one another and with Christ, we become full members of His Mystical Body and share with Him in "glory"). And the "theology" is by turns "analytic," "scriptural," and "pastoral," but rarely, as Hamlet's friend Horatio might say, is it "considering too curiously"—something that frankly does occasionally occur in the *Summa*. And happily absent from the song are the kinds of technical words that distance the doctrine from the simple understanding of the people: *transubstantio, forma et materia, substantia et accidens*.

But perhaps most strikingly, in the office for a Feast traditionally marked by processions, by the distancing of the Host in elevated, awe-inspiring, even intimidating monstrances, and by silent adoration, Aquinas throughout emphasizes instead the table and the cup, the joyful clamor of a shared feast, and the simple acts of eating bread and drinking wine. After the mention of *"pastor"* ("shepherd," but also "feeder") in the first verse, not a single subsequent verse goes by without an explicit reference to eating. And not a single verse suggests, implicitly or explicitly, anything like "silent adoration." This is what I find most re-assuring, almost radical, about the sequence—its insistence on the intimate reality of the Sacrament against the counter-pull of a distancing displacement away from the common supper-table and onto the inaccessible high altar.

Poetically, the sequence is a wonder. It is accentual and trochaic, yet can be sung to melodies composed for earlier metrical forms. It capitalizes on all the opportunities that a heavily inflected language like Latin offers for felicitous rhyme, striking word order, and verbal compression. As befits a *jubilatio* (an exultation), the stanzaic structure expands and overflows as the sequence continues, first from six- to eight-line verses, and then to a final ten-line concluding prayer. Parallelism is perhaps its most used figure, as befits a Sacrament so marked by "doubleness"—bread and wine, Body and Blood, sign and signified, human and divine, sensation and faith, here and there, now and then. The sonic repetitions, not just of the end rhymes, but of the occasional mid-rhymes, assonances, and alliterations, help to clinch the meaning. It is in places allusive as well as direct, and nuanced as well as precise. The mostly end-stopped lines, eminently singable and breathable, build neatly to their conclusions; and the occasional run-ons, where the syntax overflows the line, often at the end of a verse, change up the rhythm and help to emphasize the final rhymes of each stanza.

I continue to be amazed by its poetic density and sheer beauty. And I confess, I occasionally sing snatches of it as I walk to work. But then I tend to do that with other fragments of Gregorian chant as well. Et valde mane, Pueri hebraeorum, Victimae pascali laudes, and of course Salve Regina.

The Hymns

INTRODUCTION TO THE HYMNS

Three additional hymns for the Office of Corpus Christi are traditionally assigned to St. Thomas Aquinas: the *Pange Lingua* for Vespers; the *Sacris Solemniis* for Matins; and the *Verbum Supernum* for Lauds. Vespers, Matins, and Lauds are three separate divisions of the liturgical day—"Canonical Hours," as they are called. Vespers for a holy day is celebrated in the late afternoon of the evening before the feast; Matins is its official morning prayer, though it is often celebrated before sunrise; and Lauds—which means "praises"—is the first prayer of the bright day. According to Connelly, Aquinas fitted each of the three hymns to "its liturgical purpose" (p. 120).

Since Vespers prepares us in advance for the Feast, Thomas uses its hymn—the *Pange Lingua*—to recapitulate Christ's life from His miraculous birth to the moment of His institution of the Sacrament; then he calls upon us to revere this precious gift and also see it, through faith, not only as the critical moment when bread and wine are turned into His Body and Blood, but also when the Old Covenant yields to the New. And he ends the hymn with the traditional Trinitarian doxology (song of praise), while cleverly introducing into it the two keys words of opening of the *Lauda Sion*—"*laus et jubilatio*" ("praise and jubilation").

Since Matins is a morning office, Aquinas in his *Sacris Solemniis* calls upon us to greet the day with joy and loud praise, picking up the theme of "newness" from the end of the *Pange Lingua* and exploring it in more depth; and then he relates, in touching and dramatic detail, the Last Supper itself, of which the feast is a memorialization. Says Connelly:

> The fourth verse of this hymn gives what some think to be St. Thomas's most lovable picture of our Lord at the Supper as He begins His farewell to his disciples. (p. 117)

Also, for perhaps the only time in any of the songs, he draws a clear distinction between those who receive the Sacrament (all of us) and those whom Christ specifically appointed to administer it (priests). The *Panis Angelicus* section reiterates the wonder of the Sacrament, and the doxology links the present liturgy to the coming light of glory.

Since Lauds calls for light and clarity, Aquinas retells and extends the Last Supper narrative in his *Verbum Supernum Prodiens*, but now with a clear eye on both Christ's incarnational divinity and His impending death. Thus the Eucharist is not merely the sharing of Himself as food, it is also a memorial of His Passion—both Sacrament and sacrifice. The final verses recapitulate the chronology behind the Sacrament: Incarnation, Last Supper, Passion, Glory; and the doxology looks forward to the endless future where we shall at last find in heaven our true home.

So each hymn focuses on themes appropriate to the liturgical "Hour"; and together they create, sometimes with overlapping narratives, the full sweep of Eucharistic "history"—with the Mass of the feast and its *Lauda Sion* serving as a perfect climax. Connelly concludes his introductory remarks thus: "It is a pity that later hymn-writers, revisers and composers of offices did not learn their hymnology as well as their theology from the Angelic Doctor" (p. 118).

The Prosodic Structure of the Hymns

The *Pange Lingua* is modeled roughly on an earlier Passiontide hymn by Fortunatus with the same opening three words (Connelly, pp. 82–85). Hymnologists would identify Aquinas's version as six verses composed of three-line stanzas of trochaic tetrameter, each line with a truncated final foot (catalectic). Prosodists would call it trochaic octameter catalectic. In simpler terms, each line contains eight trochaic feet (with variations), the final foot being truncated (DUM-duh DUM-duh DUM-duh DUM-duh // DUM-duh DUM-duh DUM-duh DUM). After the first four feet of each line there is usually a slight pause (caesura, marked //). What Aquinas adds to the structure is intricate rhyming—both at the caesuras and at the ends, so that each verse actually reads like a six-line stanza rhyming AbAbAb, with the lower case 'b' indicating the line with the truncated foot. (I have been unable to duplicate the internal rhymes in my translation.)

The **Sacris Solemniis** is composed of seven verses, each verse a four-line stanza, with a very complex rhyme scheme—though actually by Anglophone standards, they are more assonances and identities than true rhymes. Metrically, it is mostly written in accentual dactylic tetrameter (DUM-duh-duh DUM-duh-duh // DUM-duh-duh DUM-duh-duh), with a caesura in the middle of the first three lines; the fourth line is short and irregular and rhymes with the first half of the third line. The last two verses of the hymn form the famous *Panis Angelicus* (Connelly, pp. 120–22).

The **Verbum Supernum** is modeled on a Advent hymn beginning with the same three words (Connelly, pp. 50–53). Prosodists would call it accentual iambic tetrameter with some variations but without a caesura (duh-DUM duh-DUM duh-DUM duh-DUM). It is composed of six verses of four-line stanzas, each stanza rhyming alternately (abab), though the fourth verse has only one rhyming sound (aaaa).

I find it intriguing that Aquinas used four different prosodic forms for all four of his songs, never repeating himself, challenging himself to master all four. Which he did.

Pange Lingua
by Thomas Aquinas

Pange, lingua, gloriósi
  Córporis mystérium,
Sanguinísque pretiósi,
  Quem in mundi prétium
Fructus ventris generósi
  Rex effúdit géntium.

Nobis datus, nobis natus
  Ex intácta Vírgine,
Et in mundo conversátus,
  Sparso verbi sémine,
Sui moras incolátus
  Miro clausit órdine.

In suprémæ nocte coenæ
  Recúmbens cum frátribus
Observáta lege plene
  Cibis in legálibus,
Cibum turbæ duodénæ
  Se dat suis mánibus.

Verbum caro, panem verum
  Verbo carnem éfficit
Fitque sanguis Christi merum,
  Et si sensus déficit,
Ad firmándum cor sincérum
  Sola fides súfficit.

Tantum ergo sacraméntum
  Venerémur cérnui:
Et antíquum documéntum
  Novo cedat rítui:
Præstet fides suppleméntum
  Sénsuum deféctui.

Pange Lingua
Translation by Dakin Matthews

Tongue, express in song this myst'ry,
  Glorious Body, precious Blood,
Which the King of every nation—
  Fruit of noble maidenhood—
Spent to buy the world's redemption,
  Poured out for all mankind's good.

He was born of untouched virgin,
  Given to us in our need;
In the world He dwelt among us,
  Scattering His word like seed,
And the last day of his dwelling
  Closed with such a wondrous deed.

On the night of His last supper
  With His brethren as He planned,
Eats the food that was required,
  Follows all the Law's command,
Then once more to feed the Dozen,
  Gives Himself with His own hand.

Bread to flesh is transformed truly
  By the word of Word enflesh'd,
Wine becomes His Blood most surely;
  And if senses fail the test,
Faith alone is all that's needed
  To confirm a sincere breast.

Bowing down then let us worship
  Such a wondrous Sacrament—
As to this new sacred ritual
  Yields the ancient Covenant.
To what's missing in our senses,
  Faith provides the supplement.

Genitóri, Genitóque
Laus et jubilátio,
Salus, honor, virtus quoque
  Sit et benedíctio:
Procedénti ab utróque
  Compar sit laudátio.

Amen. Alleluja.

Praise and jubilation ever
  To the Father and the Son,
Hail and honor, might and glory,
  Blessings be from everyone;
And to Him from Both proceeding
  Equal praise be ever done.

Amen. Alleluia.

Verse One

Pange, lingua, gloriósi
  Córporis mystérium,
Sanguinísque pretiósi,
  Quem in mundi prétium
Fructus ventris generósi
  Rex effúdit géntium.

Tongue, express in song this myst'ry—
  Glorious Body, precious Blood,
Which the King of every nation—
  Fruit of noble maidenhood—
Spent to buy the world's redemption,
  Poured out for all mankind's good.

I have to confess there is no line I struggled with as a translator more than the initial, seemingly straightforward, line of the song—all because of that first word, "*pange*." It is, I know, traditionally translated as "sing"; Edward Caswell's version, probably the best known of all the translations, starts with "Sing, my tongue, the Saviour's glory." And though there is neither "my" nor "Saviour" in the first line of the Latin, that's understandable—dense rhyming requires a fair amount of shuffling, interpolation, and paraphrasing. In the past, I always assumed it is an instruction to the singer or singers, telling them to "sing out" the details of the great mystery of the Eucharist.

But upon further research, and mulling over Caswell's "my," I have come to the conclusion that "*pange*" does not literally mean "sing." Its root meaning is to "fix or fasten something"—like driving a nail into something; its allied meanings are to "put something together," or to "reach an agreement." "Compose" ("put together") is often its first dictionary meaning, and the English word "pact" is a derivative. In classical times, it was a popular word to describe the act of writing poetry: Horace used it so in his *Ars Poetica*: "I compose marvelous poems," he boasted; "*Ego mira poemata pango*." By the Middle Ages as well, it was frequently used to describe the act of composing poetry, rarely of composing prose.

So how do we get "sing" out of that? And whose "tongue" is being told to sing? Well, here's my new take on it. Classical poets often spoke—metaphorically—of their poetry writing as "singing"; Virgil's *Aeneid* starts off with "I sing of arms and the man" ("*Arma virumque cano*"). Homer calls upon his Muse to "sing" at the opening of the *Iliad*. We still speak of music writers as "composers," after all. So "*pangere*" could be "to sing," but primarily in the sense of "compose a song"—that is, "compose some verses to be performed aloud."

So for the *Pange lingua*, I take this first phrase as a kind of classical invocation of the writer to himself, to his tongue to be precise—as other writers may have invoked their muses or complained to their hearts or chastised their pens—identifying the task at hand: write a poem, to be performed out loud, once and for all "setting down" or "nailing down" or "expressing in a fixed prosodic form" the great mystery of the Eucharist.

My further take, for which I confess I have no evidence, is that this is the first line that Thomas wrote of the four songs, and that he wrote them in order, climaxing with the Sequence. Thus, in my fantasy, the "*Pange lingua. . . mysterium*" serves in fact as his introduction to all four songs, and identifies the goal of the entire poetic opus—as if he were saying to himself, "All right, Thomas, you've analyzed and taught this mystery in prose a number of times, at great length and in fine detail, now do it in rhyming verse and make it short and singable—and beautiful!" The wonder is, he succeeded.

As for the rest of the verse there is much to marvel at. It is a fine example of what I like to call the "density" of great poetry. By density I mean that more is packed into the verse than is suggested by the mere meanings of the words, their "denotations." Their associated meanings—their "connotations," their allusions, and even their very sounds—beyond the astonishing rhyming—all add to the mix, creating a fullness and richness beyond prose.

For one small example, the tongue is not only the organ of speech, it is the bodily organ most closely associated with the reception of the Sacrament.

For another example, the opening two lines contain crucial words from the actual rite of consecration—"body," "blood," and "mystery"; recall that in Aquinas's time until midway through the twentieth century, the phrase "*mysterium fidei*" was part of the actual formula of consecration, until it was moved later and made an invitation to the congregation to respond.

For another example, the universality of the redemption effected by Christ's sacrifice is twice suggested by the words "*mundi*" and "*gentium*"—the "world" and "peoples."

For another example, the verse uses cognate words in slightly different forms—"polyptoton," for those who care about such terms—often to introduce a piquant twist to the meaning. In this first verse, Thomas speaks of Christ as the "*Rex gentium*" (King of (all) peoples), and of His mother as having a "*venter generosa*" (a noble womb). But "*Generosa*"—which in my schooldays I mistook for "generous"—actually means "high-born," and it shares the same root as "*gentium*" (*genere,* to be born); yet Mary was definitely not "high-born" by earthly standards. She was "noble" for having given birth to the King of Kings, not for the social class she was born into. (And of course the whole burden of the "*Magnificat*" is to make that very point.)

For another example, Thomas speaks of Christ's blood as precious (*pretiosi*) and then later identifies it as the price (*pretium*) paid to redeem the world, actually the "price of the world" (*pretium mundi*). Another excellent example of sharpening the meaning by the use of cognate words though their sounds, etymologies, and meanings.

For another example, the "*Fructus ventris generosi*" (fruit of a noble womb) not only recalls the *Ave Maria,* the alliteration (f-g) anticipates the same sounds in the final line (*effudit gentium*). Note also that the "*effudit*" (poured out) recalls the "*effundetur*" (will be poured out) from the Last Supper and closes the verse with yet another word from the consecration ritual.

All these rhetorical and prosodic choices create a verse bristling with meaning and allusions, like a charged electro-magnetic field. That is what I mean by density. Stephen Booth, one of my favorite Shakespearean critics, describes such poetry as a rich soup, where sharp flavors sometimes mingle and sometimes strike us with their individual sapor. Less fancifully, another critic, Karl Uitti, speaks of the effect this way:

Ambiguity enriches the meaning of the poem by creating deliberate ambivalences on all important levels of structure, characterization, and statement.

* * *

"Ambiguous" and "ambivalent" expression should not, however, be merely confusing; only the greatest artists can consistently avoid both the overly simple and the archaically indirect. (p. 163)

Two further things I find striking: in contrast to the Lauda Sion, the Incarnation is specifically referred to; and again in contrast to the Lauda Sion, unless you count "fructus"' (fruit), there are no references to food—no meat, no drink, no meal, no eating.

Verse Two

Nobis datus, nobis natus
  Ex intácta Vírgine,
Et in mundo conversátus,
  Sparso verbi sémine,
Sui moras incolátus
  Miro clausit órdine.

He was born of untouched virgin,
  Given to us in our need;
In the world He dwelt among us,
  Scattering His word like seed,
And the last day of His dwelling
  Closed with such a wondrous deed.

    The Latin of this second verse is a single sentence and an exemplar of the poet's use of sonic repetition to "fix" or "set" the meaning. It is alternately end-rhymed, of course, like all the other verses; but the opening internal rhyme (*nobis datus, nobis natus*) and the dense alliteration throughout enhance the overall effectiveness. The most prominent are the "m-c" combinations—*mundo conversatus, moras incolatus, miro clausit*. And *sparso, semine* and *virgine, verbi* add to the sense that everything fits neatly together like the pieces of a puzzle. Or, more accurately, a poem.

    Add to this the syntactical fact that the grammatical subject of the sentence, Christ, is never expressly named, but presumably borrowed from the previous verse, where he is identified as "*Rex gentium.*" In addition, the rhetorical device of placing the predicate at the very end of the sentence (periodic structure), forcing the listener to wait for it after a long series of introductory material, captures the very chronology related: given, born, consorted with us, spoke to us, waited till the very end ("*moras,*" which means roughly "the time stayed" or "time-span," has as its primary meaning "delay") to conclude "with a wonderful finale" or "with a wonderful order." And with that word "*ordo,*" it's not impossible that Aquinas may also be alluding to the institution of the priesthood ("Holy Orders") in the "order" to "do this in memory of me."

So what is the theological "thrust" of this verse? It is to briefly recapitulate the events leading up to the day of the institution of the Sacrament. "*Nobis datus*" precedes Christ's birth ("*nobis natus*") to remind us that the initiating act of the series is the Heavenly Father's "gift" of His only Begotten Son. Thomas borrows the phrasing from the earlier hymn by Fortunatus, but reverses the order to make the point. Still, that parallelism also makes it clear that the gift comes physically from Mary as well; and thus we have a second allusion linking the Eucharist to the Incarnation, this time stressing the miracle of His Virgin Birth. Yet despite His divine origin and nature, Christ not only dwelt in the world, but consorted, interacted, with it, with us. Even more, He spoke to us frequently, sowing seeds of wisdom; and then, at the very end, did more than speak—He did something truly amazing, He created something that made an "orderly" conclusion to His life. In a way Thomas's method is more "dramatic" than "theological."

It's almost like a tease. No mention yet of a meal, of food, of drink, of bread and wine, of eating. Everyone knows where this is going, yet Thomas relies upon the device of suspense to build to the climax.

Verse Three

In suprémæ nocte coenæ
  Recúmbens cum frátribus
Observáta lege plene
  Cibis in legálibus,
Cibum turbæ duodénæ
  Se dat suis mánibus.

On the night of His last supper
  With His brethren as He planned,
Eats the food that was required,
  Follows all the Law's command,
Then once more to feed the Dozen,
  Gives Himself with His own hand.

The third verse in Latin uses some of the same techniques as the first two verses, and for similar purposes. The polyptotons (*lege, legalibus; cibis, cibum*) help to "fix" the meaning firmly. The absence of an expressed subject links the three verses together, almost as if they form one long sentence. (In my translation, I have deliberately omitted the grammatical subjects.) The periodic structure—holding off the predicate "gives himself" ("*se dat*") until the last line—again creates a kind of suspense and sharpening of the focus. And then the surprise introduction of an "historical present" form of the verb—"*dat*" rather than "*dedit*"—brings the narrative suddenly alive.

Some other things to note. Thomas is probably correct in having Jesus and the disciples "reclining" (*recumbens*) for the Last Supper. Though meals eaten reclining were far more frequent among the Roman occupiers than the Jews, the Passover Seder seems to be one meal that Jews were urged to eat on special dining couches rather than chairs. In fact, special rooms were constructed with built-in reclining platforms (*triclinia*), and this is perhaps what Jesus meant when He told the disciples to find a "furnished room"— a room outfitted for dining. And we know from Luke 7:37 that when He once dined with a Pharisee, He "reclined" ("*discubuit*"). These two words were apparently so identified with dining, one did not even need to mention eating or a table.

I also like Thomas's word *"suprema"* for "last" in "Last Supper"; of course it can mean "last," but it certainly has a primary meaning of "highest," "most exalted." So again we get that poetic and productive "ambivalence" described in a previous section—as well as a near midline rhyme.

Theologically, Aquinas is making the point that Christ seems deliberately to have chosen to fulfill the requirements of the Old Covenant, following the dietary and ritualistic laws exactly, before performing the new rite that replaced them. That deliberation is something I have tried to highlight by adding the word "planned" in my translation. So the "fulfillment and replacement" aspect of the Sacrament is not just something that the Church reads back into the story of the Sacrament, but is presented as the clear intent of Christ himself at the moment of institution.

Rhetorically, this verse is a wonderful partner to the previous verse in that it continues the narrowing of topic—almost like a camera zooming in for a close-up. Verse Two, if you recall, recapitulated in six lines Christ's lifetime on earth, from His being "given" to mankind by His Father up to the "last day of His dwelling." Verse Three narrows the focus to just a single night, and then recapitulates it chronologically from the moment Christ "reclined" to eat to the exact moment He gave the Twelve "Himself" as their food. And it is at this moment that Thomas switches from past tense to the "historical present," a common technique to make the narrative feel more immediate. The next verse, as we shall see, will expand that exact moment in time, and simultaneously link it to any current moment in which the Sacrament is presented to our eyes. It's a kind of literary telescoping that brings the past so close to us that it becomes the present.

This focusing on the journey leading up to the moment of the institution of the Sacrament, this suggestion that it was deliberately "delayed" to the very last day of Christ's life, is dealt with again in the *Summa*, when Thomas asks whether it was opportune or appropriate for Christ to institute the sacrament when He did (*ST* 3.73.5). Thomas gives three reasons why he thinks it was appropriate for Christ to wait till "the last day": because He was about to leave His disciples "in His proper species, He left Himself with them under the sacramental species"; because men at all times need something to "show forth our Lord's Passion"; and because words "spoken by departing friends are committed most deeply to memory."

One might also add that the Sacrament celebrated before the actual Passion could serve as the final pre-figuring of it, even as it pre-enacted it (sacramentum et res), and thus could help the disciples understand the actual Passion when it came the next day. It seems not to have been completely successful, however, in that respect—as all the disciples fled and many were discouraged. It took Jesus's reappearance to the two disciples on the road at Emmaus and His patient recapitulation of the whole scriptural prefiguring once more before they could "recognize Him" in the "breaking of the bread" (Lk 24.13–35).

Verse Four

Verbum caro, panem verum
  Verbo carnem éfficit:
Fitque sanguis Christi merum,
  Et si sensus déficit,
Ad firmándum cor sincérum
  Sola fides súfficit.

Bread to flesh is transformed truly
  By the word of Word enflesh'd,
Wine becomes His Blood most surely;
  And if senses fail the test,
Faith alone is all that's needed
  To confirm a sincere breast.

After the narrowing, focusing, forward movement of the last two verses, Verse Four brings all to a sudden halt—like a freeze-frame—as the moment of the instituting consecration is reproduced with a density of language that makes the Latin almost untranslatable. Says Connelly: "No translation, in poetry or prose, seems quite able to meet all the antitheses of this line and a half" (p. 121). Let's see what he means by this.

First of all, Connolly is most likely speaking primarily of the first line alone, with its intricate wordplay—seven words with two instances of polyptoton (*verbum, verbo; caro, carnem*) and an alliterative and near rhyming "*verum*" thrown in for good measure. But the first "*Verbum*"— which is now a new and expressed grammatical subject—carries the special Johannine meaning of "the Word" and the first "*caro*" continues the allusion to John 1:14: "*Et verbum caro factum est*" ("And the Word was made flesh"). So now we have the third allusion to the Incarnation in so many verses, linking it to the Eucharist and emphasizing this time Christ's Divine Power—"All things were made through him" (*Omnia per ipsum facta sunt*). Then the second "*verbo*" refers to the word or words of consecration which Christ speaks over the "bread," turning it into His "flesh." It is no trick, the bread is "real," and the power of the Word's word is as great as the Creator's, who made whole worlds with a word (*Fiat lux*). So for the first time, the Sacrament is tied back even further than the Incarnation, to the Creation itself. And by the same word, wine becomes the blood of Christ. And because of the density of the expression, all seems to be occurring simultaneously.

Then halfway through the verse, the historical present seamlessly yields to the actual present and we stand before the Sacrament, and it is not just the disciples' senses that can't be trusted and their hearts that must have faith in the transformation, but our senses and our hearts as well. The poem in its own way, like the Sacrament itself, becomes a re-enactment as well as a recollection.

The construction of this verse, and of the verses carefully leading up to it, is quite breathtaking, and leads quite naturally to the call to worship and doxology that follow. And this is something we need to remember about the songs of Aquinas: they are not merely random collections of verses, but carefully laid out and organized poems, with each verse contributing sequentially, as well as thematically, to the whole.

Verses Five and Six

Tantum ergo sacraméntum
  Venerémur cérnui:
Et antíquum documéntum
  Novo cedat rítui:
Præstet fides suppleméntum
  Sénsuum deféctui.

Genitóri, Genitóque
  Laus et jubilátio,
Salus, honor, virtus quoque
  Sit et benedíctio:
Procedénti ab utróque
  Compar sit laudátio.

Bowing down then let us worship
  Such a wondrous Sacrament—
As to this new sacred ritual
  Yields the ancient Covenant.
To what's missing in our senses,
  Faith provides the supplement.

Praise and jubilation ever
  To the Father and the Son,
Hail and honor, might and glory,
  Blessings be from everyone;
And to Him from Both proceeding
  Equal praise be ever done.

These two verses are frequently detached from the full hymn and sung separately at Benediction. It is the first time that we are urged to worship or venerate the Sacrament, bowing down as we do so (*veneremur cernui*). Recall that idea of reverently worshiping the Sacrament makes no appearance in the *Lauda Sion,* which speaks initially of "praising" it, and then insistently of "eating" and "food" and "drink." The reason for the difference is what

Connelly calls the appropriateness of the hymns to their liturgical placement. The Sequence is part of the Mass, when the Sacrament is consumed; the other hymns are part of the recited or sung office, often in the presence of the Sacrament, when the host is neither consecrated nor consumed.

The last two lines of the fourth verse repeat and amplify the call to faith on the part of the believers—the necessity of faith, since the senses, dependent upon appearances (*species*), are incapable of grasping the reality (*res*) of Christ's presence. All six lines are placed in the subjunctive, rather than the indicative mood, to suggest what we *ought* to do, what we *need* to do; this verse is thus what is called "hortatory"—which is just short of imperative—"strongly urging" rather than "commanding." (I confess I have not successfully managed that tone in my translation, alas.)

But it is the middle two lines that really catch my attention—literally, "And let (an/the) old document yield to (the/a) new ritual." "*Documentum*" is derived from "*docēre*" ("to teach"), and etymologically it means "teaching" or "instruction." But by the Middle Ages it was commonly used to mean "written teaching"—our current meaning of "document." So likely what we have here is metonymy: the basic written law ("Torah") at the heart of the Old Covenant standing in for the Old Covenant itself. And the "new ritual" is also probably metonymy, the "ritual" standing in for the whole of the New Covenant. Recall that both Christ and the rite of consecration speak of the blood being of the "new covenant" ("*novi testamenti*")— "*testamentum*" again being a metonymic stand-in for the whole of the "new covenant," as well as an allusion to the act and document—the last will and testament—of "willing someone something after one's death."

What I find evocative is that one might logically expect one ritual to yield to another, or one document to another, but making a document yield to a ritual captures for me a crucial difference between the Old Covenant and the New, one that Thomas seems to be making and one that St. Paul was particularly keen on articulating—the difference between a covenant based on "law" and one based on "love," as expressed by the gift of Himself that Christ gave. (Aquinas makes this distinction much better in his Latin that I do in my English.)

The doxology of Verse Six is pretty standard fare, though it does manage, as I noted earlier, to include key words from the opening of the Lauda Sion—

"praise and jubilation" (laus et jubilatio). And of course "virtus" is not our "virtue," but "power" or "might," and is essentially a prayer—and a recognition—that God's will may prevail, for His is "the power and the glory." Amen. Alleluia.

Sacris Solemniis
By Thomas Aquinas

Sacris solémniis
  iuncta sint gáudia,
et ex praecórdiis
  sonent praecónia;
recédant vétera,
  nova sint ómnia,
corda, voces, et ópera.

Noctis recólitur
  cena novíssima,
qua Christus créditur
  agnum et ázyma
dedísse frátribus,
  iuxta legítima
priscis indúlta pátribus.

Post agnum typicum,
  explétis epúlis,
Corpus Domínicum
  datum discípulis,
sic totum ómnibus,
  quod totum síngulis,
eius fatémur mánibus.

Dedit fragílibus
  córporis férculum,
dedit et trístibus
  sánguinis póculum,
dicens: Accípite
  quod trado vásculum;
omnes ex eo bíbite.'

Sacris Solemniis
Translated by Dakin Matthews

To our most solemn feasts
  Let us join joyfulness.
Let there sound from our chests
  Heralds of happiness.
Let old things pass from view,
  Let all be made anew,
Voices, hearts, and our actions, too.

We celebrate that eve,
  That Final Supper when
Christ, as we all believe,
  Gave to his brethren
Lamb and unleavened bread,
  As their forefathers fed,
And the old Law had mandated.

Once the disciples dined,
  Once the meal was complete,
Christ—whom the lamb foresigned—
  Gave them His Flesh to eat—
As much to everyone
  As He gave anyone—
By His own hand we say 'twas done.

A dish of Flesh He shared
  For their fragility;
A cup of Blood prepared
  For their despondency;
Said to them, "Take it up,
  I give to you this cup,
From it all of you now must sup."

Sic sacrifícium
  istud instítuit,
cuius offícium
  commítti vóluit
solis presbyteris,
  quibus sic cóngruit,
ut sumant, et dent céteris.

Panis angélicus
  fit panis hóminum;
dat panis cáelicus
  figúris términum;
O res mirábilis:
  mandúcat Dóminum
pauper, servus et húmilis.

Te, trina Déitas
  únaque, póscimus:
sic nos tu vísita,
  sicut te cólimus;
per tuas sémitas
  duc nos quo téndimus,
ad lucem quam inhábitas.

So did he institute
  This holy sacrament;
And He was resolute
  That only priests were meant
To do what should be done,
  And honor His intent,
To feed themselves and everyone.

Bread fit for angels then,
  Bread down from heaven sent,
Becomes the bread of men,
  Fulfills prefigurement.
What an amazing feat!
  Master becomes the meat
Poor men, servants, and wretches eat.

Thou Godhead glorious
  Equally one and three,
We pray Thee come to us
  As we do worship Thee,
And on Thy paths lead us,
  To where we're meant to be,
Where Thou in light live eternally.

Verse One

Sacris solémniis
  iuncta sint gáudia,
et ex praecórdiis
  sonent praecónia;
recédant vétera,
  nova sint ómnia,
corda, voces, et ópera.

To our most solemn feasts
  Let us join joyfulness.
Let there sound from our chests
  Heralds of happiness.
Let old things pass from view,
  Let all be made anew,
Voices, hearts, and our actions, too.

This Matins hymn, to be sung as a morning song, immediately introduces a theme of boisterous brightness against the hushed night-time solemnity of the Vespers *Pange lingua*. Thomas urges us to join to the "solemnness" of the feast strong notes of joyfulness (*gaudia*). He uses the plural of "*praeconium*," traditionally translated as "laudation," but its etymology is rooted in the way public heralds announced their messages or auctioneers hawked their wares. And he has these "public outcries" come from deep in the chest (*praecordiis*) not from the mouth—at the same time returning to his old trick of not just end-rhyming but also of using words that sound like one another (*praeconia, praecordiis*) to strengthen the meaning. Also as befits a morning song, he highlights the "newness" of the Sacrament, now emphasizing the replacement and banishment of the "old," along with urging us to respond to it with new "hearts, voices, and acts"— with "new everything."

There is thus the clear sense that we should not try to hang onto "old things," old ways; we should "let them go" (*recedant vetera*). In his other Corpus Christi songs, the battle between the old and the new was mostly between covenants and rituals; here it seems to be focused more on the behavior of the faithful, on those preparing to receive the Sacrament that day—the belief that each new day brings a new chance to rid ourselves of old habits and acquire new ones. So once again the entire verse is subjunctive in mood and therefore "hortatory."

Thomas's rhyme scheme is complex, and I have not always been able to follow it exactly in my translation. But I have tried to capture the livelier, somewhat less solemn tone. It is morning, after all.

Verses Two and Three

Noctis recólitur
  cena novíssima,
qua Christus créditur
  agnum et ázyma
dedísse frátribus,
  iuxta legítima
priscis indúlta pátribus.

Post agnum typicum,
  explétis epúlis,
Corpus Domínicum
  datum discípulis,
sic totum ómnibus,
  quod totum síngulis,
eius fatémur mánibus.

We celebrate that eve,
  That Final Supper when
Christ, as we all believe,
  Gave to his brethren
Lamb and unleavened bread,
  As their forefathers fed,
And the old Law had mandated.

Once the disciples dined,
  Once the meal was complete,
Christ—whom the lamb foresigned—
  Gave them His Flesh to eat—
As much to everyone
  As He gave anyone—
By His own hand we say 'twas done.

These two verses, like the third and fourth verses of the *Pange lingua*, narrate the events of the Last Supper; but what Thomas does here is expand the narrative and enrich it with detail. In the *Pange lingua*, there was a swift recapitulation of the actions leading up to the consecration and then what I called a "freeze-frame" for the act itself. Here we have something more like a movie.

The feast, we are told, recalls and celebrates (*recolere*) the night of the Last Supper, but for "last" Aquinas again uses a word charged with ambivalence, "*novissima*," which only means "last" because it means the "very newest," thus continuing the theme of "newness" announced in the previous verse. And the continuing alliteration (*noctis, novissima; Christus, creditor; agnus, azyma*) once again helps to reinforce and "fix" the meaning.

But more important is the richness of detail Aquinas adds: the unleavened bread (*azyma*) and the Pascal Lamb (*agnus*) do not explicitly appear in the Gospel narrative, but it is "presumed" (*creditur*) they are there, since we are told it is a Passover seder that Christ and the Twelve are celebrating (Lk 22:7ff, Mt 26:17ff); and those were the rules imposed (*legitima indulta*) upon their Jewish forefathers (*priscis patribus*). Some of the Gospel narratives merely say "when the meal was over," but Thomas actually pictures Jesus "having given" (*dedisse*) the azymes and lamb to His brethren (*fratribus*) before moving on to the new rite.

And even when this prelude is done, when the meal is over (the alliterating *expletis epulis*), Thomas repeats the word "lamb," but now identifies it not as a symbol of the old rite (whose blood spared the Jewish firstborn in Egypt) but as a "type" (*typicum*), a prefiguring of the new, in fact the best prefiguring of the new (*ST* 3.73.6). The next line with its triple alliteration (*dominicum datum discipulis*) tells us what it is He gives to His disciples—His own body (*corpus dominicum*) with His own hands (*manibus*)—and all this is the truth that we "profess" (*fatemur*). Then in a preview of Verse Eight of the *Lauda Sion*, he adds (in the echoing "*Sic totum omnibus, qud totum singulis*") "As much to everyone / As He gave anyone" (See *ST* 3.76.3). Here we note that Aquinas has more than mere narrative in mind: he means to stir the imagination as well, and then couple that with theological precision and pastoral instruction, as he did in the *Lauda Sion*.

So the difference between the story of the Last Supper in these first two hymns is this: in the *Pange Lingua*, the institution of the Sacrament is presented as a kind of frozen moment at the end of a brief and narrowing sequence, starting as far back as the Incarnation, moving though Christ's public life, His teaching, His final meal, to focus on the instant of consecration itself. In the *Sacris Solemniis*, the Last Supper is presented almost without introduction; we are thrown, as it were, *in medias res,* and the "moving picture" is painted in rich and specific detail. It is, in its way, even dramatic.

As we shall see in the next verse, the drama will also include something we have not seen before in Aquinas's retelling of the story of the Last Supper, the play of human emotions—not just of the disciples, but of Jesus himself.

Verse Four

Dedit fragílibus
  córporis férculum,
dedit et trístibus
  sánguinis póculum,
dicens: Accípite
  quod trado vásculum;
omnes ex eo bíbite.'

A dish of Flesh He shared
  For their fragility;
A cup of Blood prepared
  For their despondency;
Said to them, "Take it up,
  I give to you this cup,
From it all of you now must sup."

My translation is somewhat loose here, so for the record the Latin says literally:

He gave to the weak
  A little dish of (His) body;
He gave to the sad,
  A little cup of (His) blood,
Saying, "Take
  This little vessel I'm handing over;
All of you, drink from it."

There is a familiarity in the diminutives applied to all the tableware (no "chalices" here) that gives the scene a kind of intimacy. But more importantly, Thomas injects real emotion into the action. On the material level, of course, bread is traditionally thought to give "strength," and wine to give "cheer"; therefore quite literally, the first serves the weak and the second, the sad or downcast. But Aquinas, I think, implies something more—Christ's fore-knowledge that His Passion will weaken and sadden His disciples; and so the institution of the Sacrament at His last meeting with them, besides being the foundational rite of the New Covenant, is also an expression of His deep care for them, as they are about to face the greatest challenge to their faith.

This is clearly in line with Thomas's suggestion in the *Summa* that Christ may have "appropriately" chosen His final day for the institution of the Sacrament partially out of care for His "brothers" whom He was about to leave and to whom He wished to give a parting gift of Himself and the strongest possible memory (*ST* 3.7.3). The result is a scene suffused with emotion, and as Connelly describes it, perhaps "the most lovable picture of our Lord at the Supper as He begins to say His farewell to the disciples" (p. 117).

I feel the following verses demonstrate a double "shifting of gears," as Thomas reverts to a more theological and pastoral analysis and then, with the "Panis Angelicus," provides that amazing summary of Eucharistic doctrine I wrote about extensively in the Introduction (pp. 23–26).

Verse Five

Sic sacrifícium
  istud instítuit,
cuius offícium
  commítti vóluit
solis presbyteris,
  quibus sic cóngruit,
ut sumant, et dent céteris.

So did he institute
  This holy sacrament;
And He was resolute
  That only priests were meant
To do what should be done,
  And honor His intent,
to feed themselves and everyone.

Again, this is a rather loose translation; so here it is literally:

Thusly this sacrifice
He instituted,
Whose office
He wished to be given
To priests alone,
For whom it was/is fitting
To receive (it) and give (it) to others.

The use of the word "*congruit*" ("is/was fitting") suggests a couple of things. The first is that because both the present and the perfect tense are the same form, it can be read as either past or present—probably both. And this creates a kind of fusion of the past and the present, so that the Apostles at the Last Supper are linked with the priests of Thomas's day (and ours), who continue to celebrate the Sacrament of the Eucharist, first obliged to partake of the host themselves (*sument*), then to pass it on to others (*dent ceteris*). We have seen this fusion of past and present before in Thomas's Eucharistic poetry, and indeed noted that it mirrors a similar fusion of past and present time that takes place in the very celebration of the Sacrament itself, both a "commemoration" and an actual liturgical re-enacting (*colere*).

And secondly, "*congruit*" in the context of a statement about the priesthood essentially reminds us of the "fitness" that only priests should administer the sacrament, a fitness that Thomas insists was Christ's intention from the beginning (*officium committi **voluit** solis presbyteros*). That "fitness" calls to mind Aquinas's whole theology of the priesthood. He deals with the issue briefly in Question 82 of the *Summa*: "Of the ministers of this sacrament," specifically in Articles One and Three (*ST* 3.82.1 and 3). But because he died before finishing his masterwork, we must turn to the earlier *Summa Contra Gentiles* for a fuller treatment of "Holy Orders" (*ScG* 4.56 and 74; pp. 246–48 and 285–88).

I don't intend to survey it all here, just note some highlights. The Eucharist is the most noble and complete of all the sacraments, therefore the powers of ordination "must be weighed chiefly by reference to this sacrament" (*ScG* 4.74.6, pp. 287–88). For Aquinas, the fitness of men for this office—at his time as now, only men could be priests—also stems from the fact that of all the sacraments, this is the only one in which the minister acts, as it were, in "the person of Christ" ("*in persona Christi*"), while in other sacraments the minister speaks in his own person (*ST* 3.83.3 and elsewhere). And acting "*in persona Christi*," the priest should do as Christ did, consecrate it in order to "give it to others" (*ST* 3.83.3).

It is also Thomas's belief, even lacking explicit scriptural evidence, that the sacrament of Orders was instituted at the same time as that of the Eucharist, since at the moment of institution of the sacrament Christ simultaneously ordered it "to be frequented"—which would have been impossible for a Church that was promised to last till the end of time, unless the power of passing on the power of consecration to future generations were included. So it was only "fitting" that that power—"to ordain"—be imparted, and that it be itself a sacrament (*ScG* 4.74.2 and 3, pp. 286–87). In other words, he makes a logical argument from "congruence" rather than one drawn from scripture. Finally, the word "orders" itself suggests a kind of congruence, a fitting of the office to the power attached to the office (*ScG* 4.75.1, p. 288).

This verse, for me, pales somewhat after the intense beauty of the previous three, but apparently Thomas felt it was important to make with utter clarity the legal, procedural, and pastoral case for how the Eucharist was to be administered. I am grateful that in the sumptuous "Panis angelicus" that follows, the poet in him returns in fine, breathtaking lyric form.

Verses Six and Seven

Panis angélicus
  fit panis hóminum;
dat panis cáelicus
  figúris términum;
O res mirábilis:
  mandúcat Dóminum
pauper, servus et húmilis.

Te, trina Déitas
  únaque, póscimus:
sic nos tu vísita,
  sicut te cólimus;
per tuas sémitas
  duc nos quo téndimus,
ad lucem quam inhábitas.

Bread fit for angels then,
  Bread down from heaven sent,
Becomes the bread of men,
  Fulfills prefigurement.
What an amazing feat!
  Master becomes the meat
Poor men, servants, and wretches eat.

Thou Godhead glorious
  Equally one and three,
We pray Thee come to us
  As we do worship Thee,
And on Thy paths lead us,
  To where we're meant to be,
Where Thou in light live eternally.

In my introduction, I wrote at some length about Verse Six; so I refer
the reader there for my comments on the *Panis angelicus* lines. What is of

interest to me here is Verse Seven, the doxology, which unlike that of the *Pange lingua*, is anything but standard fare. Let us look at it a little more closely.

It starts with the usual Trinitarian formula of "Three-in-One," but instead of being a poem of praise, it is one of prayer or pleading (*poscimus*). And what is asked for is not all that simple. The first request is for God to "visit us"; but that is (somewhat surprisingly) qualified with a conditional—"visit us *as* we worship You" (*sicut te colimus*). And that word for worship is a familiar one from the phrase "*recolitur memoria*"—which we have already determined means something more than "remember," more like "celebrate and re-enact the memory." In addition, the phrasing cannot but remind us of a similar phrase in the Lord's Prayer—"forgive us *as* we forgive." So does the prayer suggest—or better, acknowledge—that God's coming to us may be in some way "dependent" upon our performing the necessary rituals? In the context of the Feast of Corpus Christi, does this mean that our obedience to Christ's command "Do this in memory of me," is not optional but a condition of our union with Him—in short, necessary for salvation?

The one thing we need to avoid is any kind of "ritual automatism"—the belief that our rituals *force* God or "the gods" to behave a certain way. We still "plead" (*poscimus*) for Him to come and be with us (*nos visita*). All of Thomas's theology, as well as his songs, stress the fact that the Eucharist, like the Incarnation, is God's free gift to us, and that the graces that flow from any sacramental act are unearned and undeserved. If there is obligation, it flows the other way; we perform this new commemorative rite in gratitude for the free gift; "Eucharist," after all, means "thanksgiving."

Still, the question does arise, and Thomas deals with it specifically in the *Summa*: "Whether the Eucharist is necessary for salvation?" (*ST* 3.73.3). His answer is a qualified "no," at least not in the same way baptism is; but how he gets to that "no" is an illuminating journey. The catalyst for his negative response is Augustine's assurance that parents need not "suppose that children cannot possess life, who are deprived of the body and blood of Christ." He is speaking here of "eternal life" and of baptized children who die young, before they receive their "first communion." Of course, he says consolingly, they can be saved.

Admittedly, there can be no salvation, Thomas says, without the "unity of the mystical body," which is the ultimate "reality" (*res*) of the Eucharistic *sacramentum*. But as in Baptism, "a man can obtain salvation though the desire of receiving it," which theologians have ever since called "the baptism of desire" (*baptismum in voto*).

But the link between the two sacraments is even stronger for Aquinas. In his formulation, Baptism *incorporates* one into the Mystical Body, and the Eucharist *perfects* one in it. In fact, through Baptism man is "ordained" (*ordinatur*) for the Eucharist—or as we might say, "oriented" or "destined" for it—in such a way that it creates an implicit desire for the Eucharist, a desire which may be expressed in a baptized adult and tacit in children, who nonetheless are granted it "through the Church's intention" (*ex intentione Ecclesiae*), just as faith was granted to them in their infant baptism "though the faith of the Church" (*ex fide Ecclesiae*).

What I find most provocative here is this idea of being "ordained" or being "oriented" or "destined" for salvation in the Mystical Body: the suggestion that "the end" is somehow contained in "the desire"—or "the goal" somehow present in "the journey." Thomas elsewhere speaks of the special grace of the sacrament imprinting a "character" upon the recipient, "adepting" (*adeptio*) him for glory (*ST* 3.79.2). Many translations adopt "attainment" as the meaning of "*adeptio*," but surely it is more like "make one capable of," or "make glory an attainable end for him." Or in colloquial terms, "put him on the path to glory."

And this is how I make sense of the next two lines, that ask God literally to "lead us where we are tending" (*duc nos quo tendimus*). I love the complexity that lies under that simplicity. It is first another possible allusion to the Lord's prayer—"lead us" is the very next petition after "forgive us as we forgive." In fact, the prayer of the doxology may be unconsciously modeled on the Our Father: we offer God worship; we ask Him to come to earth (not just His kingdom and His will): we ask Him to lead us (though *to* something rather than *away from* something—to Heaven, rather than away from temptation and evil); and, implicitly, the bread we beg for is not our daily fare but the Bread of Angels.

But more importantly, these last two lines encapsulate the whole idea that the grace of the Sacrament has put man on the right path (*semita*), one that ends in glory; has even made him "adept" at experiencing a foretaste of the glory, provided in the form of sustenance along the way (*viaticum*), until he reaches the end of his journey, which is "the light" where God lives (*lucem quam inhabitas*). So the morning song ends where it should—with the coming of the light.

So where the Pange lingua linked the Incarnation and the Eucharist and called us to worship, the Sacris Solemniis strongly re-emphasizes the intimate and immediate reality of the Last Supper and specifically reinforces the "eating" theme, as we draw nearer to the time for the celebration of the Corpus Christi Mass. I also love the "directionality" of the final verse: we beg God to **come down** *and visit us, so that He may* **lead us back up** *to where we, by His presence, are now able to go, to the heaven of light and glory, which the closing of the next hymn will punningly call our "patria"—both "the Father's home" and, as adopted and "adepted" children, our "fatherland."*

Verbum Supernum Prodiens
By Thomas Aquinas

Verbum Supernum Prodiens
Translated by Dakin Matthews

Verbum supérnum pródiens,
Nec Patris linquens déxteram,
Ad opus suum éxiens,
Venit ad vitæ vésperam.

The Word, as He set forth from
 Heaven—
Yet never from the Father's side—
To do the task that he was given,
Came to his own life's eventide.

In mortem a discípulo
Suis tradéndus áemulis,
Prius in vitæ férculo
Se trádidit discípulis.

To death about to be betrayed
By a disciple, to his foes,
A dish of life he thereon made
And gave Himself to those he chose.

Quibus sub bina spécie
Carnem dedit et sánguinem;
Ut dúplicis substántiæ
Totum cibáret hóminem.

His Flesh He gave them and His Blood
Under a double countenance,
For twofold man a twofold food,
To give the whole man sustenance.

Se nascens dedit sócium,
Convéscens in edúlium,
Se móriens in prétium,
Se regnans dat in práemium.

By birth, Himself our friend he made,
At supper made Himself our food,
Dying, Himself the price He paid,
Reigning, Himself our final good.

O salutáris hóstia,
Quæ cæli pandis óstium,
Bella premunt hostília;
Da robur, fer auxílium.

O Sacrifice that sets us free,
You open wide the heavenly doors,
Bring us both strength and remedy,
Amidst these fierce and pressing wars.

Uni trinóque Dómino
Sit sempitérna glória:
Qui vitam sine término
Nobis donet in pátria.

To God Who is both One and Three,
Be praise and glory endlessly,
And in our Father's home may He
Give life to us eternally.

Verse One

Verbum supérnum pródiens,
Nec Patris linquens déxteram,
Ad opus suum éxiens,
Venit ad vitæ vésperam.

The Word, as He set forth from Heaven—
Yet never from the Father's side—
To do the task that he was given,
Came to his own life's eventide.

This Lauds hymn, the final song before the celebration of the Corpus Christi Mass, begins with a new recapitulation of the timeline leading up to the Last Supper. It is breathtakingly brief. It begins where the Gospel of John begins—"In the beginning was the Word." "*Supernum*" literally means "on high," with the connotation of "heavenly or celestial"; so what we have in "*prodiens*" is probably referring to Christ as the Son of God "going forth" to become man—which the Creed expresses as a descent from heaven (*descendit de caelis*). Yet lest this be read as a lowering of dignity or loss of divinity, Thomas is careful to add, "and not leaving the Father's right hand" (*Nec patris liquens dexteram*). This is, by the way, a deliberate change from the earlier hymn (with the same title) on which he based his "*Verbum Supernum*." That earlier Advent hymn has the Word "leaving the bosom of the eternal Father" ("*prodiens / E patris aeterni sinu*") (Connelly, p. 50).

The next two lines find Christ both "going out" (*exiens*) and "coming" (*venit*). It seems clear that the meaning "going out to His work" (*Ad opus suum exiens*) is "leaving (heaven) to (do) His work (on earth)," though there might be a slight undertone of "on the way out to meet His death"—which is clearly the tenor of the second verse. And then suddenly, the years are collapsed, in what Shakespeare calls "jumping o'er time," and we are, without warning, at the last night of Jesus's life.

This is so unlike a similar passage in the *Pange lingua*, where the span between Incarnation and the Last Supper is chronicled in increasingly specific detail. And it is equally unlike the way the Supper is described (in quite graphic detail) in the *Sacris Solemniis* with no introductory chronology at all, pretty much just a "remember the night." Here in the *Verbum Supernum*, history seems to break in unexpectedly on eternity.

Aquinas achieves the effect through a number of syntactical and rhetorical strategies. First, the sentence is a "periodic" one—that is, the main clause is held to the very end, preceded by three parallel introductory phrases. And those three phrases are built around present participles (*prodiens, liquens, exiens*), all giving impression of present, ongoing activity. And all three deliberately stress a kind of divine eternal present: the Word is setting forth, but not leaving, is going—and then suddenly He *comes/came* (*venit*)—probably past tense—to the final night of His life, described as His "vespers" (a ritual hour)—whose initial "*v*" is anticipated by "*venit*" and "*vitae*" in this line and the "*Verbum*" that opens the verse, all the alliteration fixing in place the exact moment of that past event. And it is not just the night of His last day, it is the evening of His life (*vitae vesperam*).

I think the sense of "shock" is intentional: the staggering paradox that this divine eternal Being is suddenly facing the last night of His life on earth is exactly what Thomas is trying, for the first time in any of the songs, to convey; and like a good poet, he not only "conveys" it with the meaning of the words, he re-creates the effect through their rhythms and sounds as well.

Verse Two

In mortem a discípulo
Suis tradéndus áemulis,
Prius in vitæ férculo
Se trádidit discípulis.

To death about to be betrayed
By a disciple, to his foes,
A dish of life he thereon made
And gave Himself to those he chose.

After the "*vitae vesperam*" of the previous verse, the "*Ad mortem*" that starts the first line of the second verse casts a real chill. Death intrudes on eternal life, with only a single evening parting them.

The entire verse is a model of poetic antithesis, the structural pitting of part against part and idea against idea. The first two lines are set against the last two. The disciples are set against the envious rivals (*aemulis*). Life is set against death. And one kind of handing over (*tradere*) is set against another kind, with one more instance of polyptoton cementing the meaning (*tradendus, tradidit*; "about to be handed over"; "he handed over").

And in the verse we seem again to enter the mind of Jesus, as we did in the middle verses of the *Sacris Solemniis*, where He seemed to be expressing His concern for His disciples' vulnerability and sadness. It is not just that He is about to be handed over by one of them to His enemies; it is that He knows this, even says it to them (Mt 26:14–25; Mk 24:17–21; Lk 22:21–23; Jn 13:21–30). And still He gives Himself.

Interestingly, the evangelists present us with slightly different chronologies. Matthew and Mark place both the announcement of the betrayal and the Eucharist "while they were at supper"—the announcement coming before the "consecration." Luke seems to place both just after the supper, the Eucharist before the announcement. And John, who astonishingly does not narrate the institution of the Eucharist, seems to place the announcement either during or after the supper—it is hard to say which—but also makes a point of emphasizing Christ's fore-knowledge of Judas's impending betrayal, indeed seems to make it the motivation for much of His discourse to His disciples and for His washing of their feet:

> Before the feast of the Passover, Jesus, knowing that the hour had come for him to pass out of this world to the Father, having loved his own who were in the world, loved them to the end.
>
> And during the supper, the devil having already put it into the heart of Judas Iscariot, the son of Simon, to betray him, Jesus, knowing that the Father had given all things into his hand, and that he had come forth from God and was going to God, rose from the supper and laid aside his garments, and taking a towel girded himself. Then he poured water into the basin and began to wash the feet of the disciples, and to dry them with the towel with which he was girded. (Jn 13:1–5)

I quote this at some length because it leads me to believe that Aquinas had John's account in mind when he wrote this part of the hymn—even though John does not narrate the institution of the Eucharist. First of all, Thomas does identify Christ as "the Word" in the first line of the hymn, a Johannine expression that emphasizes His timeless divinity. Then John uses the phrases "came forth from God and was going to God"—which also sounds a lot like the first three lines of the hymn. But mostly because what John highlights beyond Christ's divine nature is His human love and care for His disciples just as He is about to leave them, even knowing—in spite of knowing—that one of them will betray Him to His enemies.

This generosity of spirit, both divine and human, extends, I think, to become the central theme of this hymn: Christ's loving gift of Himself. Indeed, Connelly points out that some form of "giving" appears in every verse but the first (p. 125).

The Sunday I wrote this section, the first reading at Mass was from Wisdom 18:6–9:

> *The night of the Passover was known beforehand to our fathers, that, with sure knowledge of the oaths in which they had put their faith, they might have courage. Your people awaited the salvation*

of the just and the destruction of their foes. For when you punished our adversaries, in this you glorified us you had summoned. For in secret the holy children of the good were offering sacrifice and putting into effect with one accord the divine institution. (From Lectionary 117 for the Nineteenth Sunday in Ordinary Time; other translations may differ.)

What struck me about the first three sentences was the stark difference between the Old Pasch and the New, between those who believe God wants them to rejoice over the destruction of their enemies, and the God who loves His betrayer and urges us to love our enemies, Who gives so much of Himself to all mankind, because "God so loved the world that he gave His only-begotten Son" (Jn 3:16); and that Son in turn gave us all the gift of Himself (Se tradidit). And specifically at the Last Supper, John seems to be insisting, the impulse to give was human as well as divine. He "loved them to the end."

Verse Three

Quibus sub bina spécie
Carnem dedit et sánguinem;
Ut dúplicis substántiæ
Totum cibáret hóminem.

His Flesh He gave them and His Blood
Under a double countenance,
For twofold man a twofold food,
To give the whole man sustenance.

Aquinas links this verse to the preceding through the relative pronoun "*quibus*" ("to whom"); so the first two lines, set in the past (*dederit*, gave), refer specifically to the disciples. But the next two lines are set in the imperfect subjunctive ("*cibaret,*" "would feed" rather than "fed") so once again we experience—in the hymn just as in the sacrament itself—the simultaneity of the past and the present, and the fusion between a specific "group of twelve" (*turba duodena*) and the universal "mankind" (*hominem*).

And the "double appearance" (*bina specie*) of the Sacramental sign—divided into "flesh and blood" (*carnem et sanguinem*)—may signify, on the material level, that man needs both food and drink to stay alive, but it simultaneously acknowledges that man himself is a kind of double substance (*duplicis substantiae*), has a kind of double nature—that is, of flesh and spirit, body and soul; and therefore a Sacrament that feeds the whole man (*totum hominem*) by offering material nourishment in its sign (*sacramentum*) while in fact supplying spiritual nourishment in its reality (*res*) is particularly "appropriate." Remember it is a basic principle of Thomas's sacramental theology that "The spiritual life is analogous to the corporeal life, since corporeal things bear a resemblance to the spiritual" (*ST* 3.73.1).

And it may not be too great a stretch to suggest that Christ's own personal experience of man's binary nature (*duplex substantia*), His human empathy with His fellow man, even His very personal love of His disciples (as John clearly suggests), contributed, along with His divine love, to His institution of this Sacrament the night before He died. That the pain of separation was not all on the disciples' side. "Jesus wept" (Jn 11:35).

I think this is one of the particular beauties of this hymn—as it is of John's gospel—its emphasis on Christ's human emotions, even as it asserts His divine knowledge and will, so that the Sacrament of "love" as Thomas sometimes calls it, includes human love as well—His and ours. The "love one another as I have loved you" is not just an ethical principle, it is a Sacramental reality. And He loved us in His "double nature" too, both as man and as God.

Verse Four

Se nascens dedit sócium,
Convéscens in edúlium,
Se móriens in prétium,
Se regnans dat in práemium.

By birth, Himself our friend he made,
At supper made Himself our food,
Dying, Himself the price He paid,
Reigning, Himself our final good.

Another perfect fusion of meaning and style. Another striking variation in constructing the song and telling the story. Each hymn has at it center, a re-telling of the institution of the Sacrament. In the *Pange lingua*, Thomas uses a brief chronology of Christ's life on earth as a lead-up to the night of the Last Supper. In the *Sacris Solemniis*, the Last Supper is narrated in great and moving detail, but virtually without any prior chronology. And in this hymn, it is the Word's divine pre-existence with God and His imminent departure to earth that suddenly "jumps o'er time," like a "smash-cut" in a film, to the night before His death. And then, only after the narration of that supper, do we get the chronology, but as a summary rather than an introduction—and a summary totally governed by the act of "self-giving."

Copying almost exactly the structure of the first verse—three present participles (*nascens, convescens, moriens*) followed by the main clause (*se regnans dat in premium*)—the poet also plays, as he did in the first verse, with time sequence—or more accurately, with shifting tense. "*Se dedit*" ("He gave himself"), though it is expressed only once, governs the three first lines. In a literal translation:

Being born, he gave himself (as our) comrade,
Dining, (he gave himself) as the food,
Dying (he gave) himself as the price. . . .

Then, suddenly, we are no longer in the past, but Christ "reigning, *gives* himself as the reward." This is just the reverse of the movement in the first verse from the eternal present to the last evening of Christ's life; here the past birth, life, and death of Christ yield to the present pledge of eternity in the reward He offers, Himself in glory—both in His Glorified Body now in the Eucharist, but also in the deeper reality of the Mystical Body of believers, both now and eventually in heaven. And the present tense further suggests each time the Eucharist is celebrated, that self-giving is not just recalled but re-created, not just as a symbol, but as a reality.

Notice also the cleverness of the prosody and rhetorical figures. The strict parallelism of the clauses is echoed by repetition of the reflexive "*se*" and the participial endings in all four (*-ens, -ans*), as well as by the singleness rather than the alternation of the rhyme, unique to this verse—all the lines ending in "*-ium*." The sonic similarity of "*nascens*" and "*convescens*" and of "*pretium*" and "*premium*" have the effect of further "fixing" the meaning by the near sameness of their sounds. And of course the shift from past to present is accomplished by the polyptoton of "*dedit, dat*"—the only two finite verbs in the verse, both forms of "*dare*" (to give).

The economy and symmetry and sheer grace of the Latin are once again too fine for me to catch in the net of English.

Verses Five and Six

O salutáris hóstia,
Quæ cæli pandis óstium,
Bella premunt hostília;
Da robur, fer auxílium.

Uni trinóque Dómino
Sit sempitérna glória:
Qui vitam sine término
Nobis donet in pátria.

O Sacrifice that sets us free,
You open wide the heavenly doors,
Bring us both strength and remedy,
Amidst these fierce and pressing wars.

To God Who is both One and Three,
Be praise and glory endlessly,
And in our Father's home may He
Give life to us eternally.

Once again, Aquinas the poet works another variation, this time in how he closes the third hymn. The first ended with a doxology; the second, with a prayer. The third ends with both, first a prayer and then a doxology, each governed by the idea of "giving"— "*donet*" ("may he give") in the first stanza and "*da*" ("give") in the second. So the concluding verses continue the theme of giving right to the end.

In Verse Five, Aquinas pushes the alternate rhyming scheme about as far as it can go, not only chiming the *ends* of lines, but *beginning* the chiming words with very similar sounds in a kind of virtuosic assonant punning (*hostia, ostium, hostilia, auxilium*). Each word, despite sounding very much like all the others, means something very different (victim, gate, enemy, aid). At the same time, the first two lines, with their offer of entrance into heaven where Christ stands "opening the gate," are contrasted with the last two, where wars "press in" on earth, and the final appeal to Him is not just to "give" strength, but to "bring" assistance, implying His coming to, and presence on, the earth where the wars are raging. So in a sense, that same duality of Christ being simultaneously in heaven and on earth that was raised in the first verse, is repeated here in the next-to-last.

Then the doxology, after the typical Trinitarian invocation, asks God to bring us to the "sempiternal glory" (*sempiterna gloria*), where, the wars (*bella*) being over, He my give us "life without end" (*vitam sine termino*) in the "fatherland" (*patria*)—meaning both where the Father dwells, but also a place which we may now claim as our "homeland," since Baptism and Eucharist have both "adepted" us to it, put us on the path to it, and made us "co-heirs" of it with the Son. And there is a wonderful closure here, since the song ends where it began, with the Father in eternity.

I have thus far stressed how this hymn combines a sense of eternity with the touching narrative of Christ's love for His disciples on the final night of His life at the Last Supper. I found evidence in this heady combination, of the likely influence of the Evangelist John on Aquinas as he wrote the hymn. In the next section, I want to explore another Johannine influence, the theme of Christ's "journey of salvation."

A final thought about the *Verbum Supernum.*

I have spoken already how in the very opening of the hymn, the use of John's term "*Verbum*" ("the Word") for Christ, which Aquinas also used in Verse Four of the *Pange lingua*, should probably prepare us for a Johannine take on the Eucharist. And I think we find it in the powerful fusion of Christ's eternal divine existence and His touching human love.

But there is another Johannine theme I think we sometimes underappreciate, and that is his view of Christ's saving action as a "journey"—more specifically as a kind of "round trip" from heaven to earth and back again. I am speaking of a "coming from and going back to the Father" theme— or more accurately, a "down and up" theme—in Christ's life, to which we perhaps pay less attention than we should—though the Creeds we say at Mass make it almost impossible to miss.

The Nicaean Creed starts, as this final hymn does, with the Lord Jesus Christ (*Dominum Jesum Christum*) being "born of the Father before all ages" (*ex Patre natum ante omnia secula*). Then He "descends/descended from heaven" (*descendit de caelis*), also as in the hymn, to be born of Mary, and to die. Then the Apostles' Creed adds another "descent" after His death, a troubling one—into "Hell." (I recall my Manhattan pastor, the late great Father Peter Colapietro, grumbling from the pulpit one day when he was called upon to explain it, "They coulda left *that* one out.") Then in both creeds, Christ "rose" from the dead, then "ascended/ascends into heaven, sits at right hand of the Father" (*Et ascendit in caelum, sedet ad dexteram Patris*) (*MR*, p. 291).

All this down-and-up movement is important to our understanding of Christ's saving mission. The "descending" while "never leaving the Father's side" stresses both His divinity and what Paul, perhaps citing an already existing hymn, calls His "emptying of himself" ("*kenosis*" in Philippians 2:7). His descent into Mary's womb emphasizes His humanity; His descent into the grave emphasizes the reality of His death. His further descent into Hell ("*sheol*") was commonly read in the early Church as a kind of "rescue mission" to break open the gates of hell ("the harrowing of hell") to free the patriarchs, offering them their path to glory (*CCC*.1.5.633). Then His "rise from the dead" and His "ascension into heaven," to sit again at the right hand of the Father, not only opens the gates there (as the hymn says), but allows "the Word" to resume His proper place, now glorified with the "glory he had before" (Jn 17:5), where He can "draw all things to him" (Jn 12:32).

How does the Sacrament fit into this "journey narrative"? It seems to me that for Aquinas, the Eucharist exists as a kind of dynamic "still point" on the journey (to borrow a phrase from T. S. Eliot), a moment that captures both His imminent departure and His urgent desire to present His disciples (and us) the gift of Himself. It is a sign of His *absence*, commemorating His death; of His *presence* in His glorified resurrected Body; and of the *future* glory that waits all those who are perfected in that Mystical Body by the Sacrament. Yet our "journey" is still in progress, while His has ended. And the Eucharist provides food for that journey, which began for us after we ourselves "descended" into Christ's death in Baptism and "rose up" out of the water onto a new path to glory (Romans 6:4).

AFTERWORD

I have tried to write primarily of Thomas Aquinas as a poet, but of course it was as a theologian that he was tasked by the pope to write poetry—which he did with amazing grace and style. Turning theology into poetry requires a kind of "alchemy"—not because theology is a "baser metal," but because great poetry needs to have both the value and the beauty of pure gold. Turning Latin poetry into English verse requires another kind of translational "alchemy"; but in trying to do so, I fear I have fallen, as they say, "between two stools." Some readers may find my verse too colloquial; some may find my prosodic analyses too academic; some may find my theological analyses too obscure and my musings too personal. To all I say, glean what you can.

My initial impulse was simply to translate songs I loved in Latin into texts that could be sung in English, without losing too much of their beauty of form or density of meaning. But as I said earlier, my shortcomings—shortcomings perhaps native to modern English—made commentary and analysis necessary. And that meant something more than a purely poetic appreciation; it also involved using the hymns as Thomas himself intended, as teaching tools. And as occasions for pondering and meditation. So I think the patient reader can find much to appreciate, despite these shortcomings.

On another note, I would never deny anyone the real satisfaction and consolation, both sensual and spiritual, they might gain from hearing or singing Thomas's original songs in their original language or their traditional Gregorian chant settings. Or, for that matter, any traditional Latin texts, sung or spoken, in any liturgical context. It must be obvious by now that that has been an experience I have shared both deeply and often myself. And I continue to relish the bits of Hebrew (*hosannah, halleluia*), Greek (*kyrie eleison*), and Latin (*Agnus Dei*) my parish congregation sings every Sunday in our English language Masses.

At the same time my love of Thomas's Latin lyrics or their chant settings need not mark me as a "traditionalist." I do not love them either because they are old or because they are remote or because they are in a tongue that few understand. I love them primarily because they are beautiful in form and rich in meaning. Their age and history only add to their value in the sense that when something is that old and that honored, and still speaks to us today, it proves itself a "classic" and worth keeping. And, when necessary, translating—if possible, in a way that makes them still singable to traditional chant melodies.

But their full beauty and richness are today denied the vast majority of worshipers who can no longer appreciate them in their original tongue. I remind myself that not only is Latin virtually inaccessible to the vast majority of believers, it is itself already at two removes from Jesus's Aramaic and the Bible's Greek. And I remind myself further that the Bible's Greek is "*koine*" (the "common" language of the people) and its Latin is "the vulgate" (also the "common" language of the people). And that translation, as it technically may move away from the original, moves closer to the people. And that, too, is a very strong tradition in the Church.

So there is nothing inherently more sacred about the Latin, except for what we ascribe to it, now because of its "traditional" use in our rituals, perhaps because of an "aestheticism" that suits certain tastes, and sometimes precisely because of its "otherness" and its very unintelligibility—which, frankly, I do not feel are values that offset the loss of meaningful availability to the vast majority of the faithful.

Traditional rituals are part of all religions, as routines and habits are authentically part of all human lives; and as such they deserve to be honored and preserved. But they do have the danger, as they lose their contact with common understanding, of calcifying into something like superstitions, and turning communal events into coterie celebrations. They may emphasize distance over nearness, the arcane over the available, "showing" over "sharing"—which has always been a danger in Eucharistic celebrations with their "monstrances" and "*ostentoria*," ("*monstrare, ostentare*"; "to show")— a danger which Thomas seems almost entirely to have avoided in his hymns. And sadly, like virtually all good things human, even the finest traditional rituals can be "weaponized" to divide the people of God from one another. And when that happens to the Eucharist, we have what Thomas calls the greatest sacrilege of all, "lying to the Sacrament" by claiming a communion that one's action denies.

There are two legends about St. Thomas I would like to share. One is that when he and St. Bonaventure, who had also been tasked with writing an office for the feast, were sitting together waiting for their audience with the pope, Bonaventure read Thomas's office, promptly tore his own up, and left the room demoralized. In my lesser task of translating Thomas's work, I have often deeply sympathized with Bonaventure.

The other legend is that at the end of Thomas's life, his assistant found him unable to write any more and muttering, "All I have written seems to me to be no more than straw." But I would hope upon further reconsideration of his songs, he might humbly admit that they at least were not straw, but something like spun gold.

One more story. It is said that when Flannery O'Connor was complimented at a New York cocktail party on Catholicism's rich "symbolism" in the Eucharist, she was reported to have replied, "Well, if it's just a symbol, to hell with it."

SELECTED BIBLIOGRAPHY

_____. *Biblia Sacra juxta Vulgatam Clementinam*. Edited by Alberto Colunga and Laurentio Turrado. Matriti: Biblioteca de Autores Cristianos, 1946.

_____. *Catechism of the Catholic Church*. Mahwah, NJ: Paulist Press, 1994.

_____. *Catholic Encyclopedia*. New York: Appleton, 1907–1912. Online edition at catholic.com

_____. *Holy Bible*. New Catholic Edition. New York: Catholic Book Publishing Company, 1952.

_____. *The Jerusalem Bible*. Reader's Edition. Garden City: Doubleday, 1968.

_____. *Liber Usualis*. Tournai: Desclée and Socii, 1947.

_____. *Novi Testamenti Biblia Graeca et Latina*. 3rd ed. Edited by Joseph M. Bover. Matriti: 1953.

_____. *Missale Romanum*. Marietti: Torino, 1950.

Apel, Willi. *Gregorian Chant*. Bloomington: Indiana University Press, 1958.

Aquinas, Thomas. *On The Truth of the Catholic Faith: Summa Contra Gentiles*. 5 vols. Edited and translated by Vernon J. Bourke. Garden City: Image, 1956.

_____. *Summa Theologiae*. 5 vols. Ottawa: Commissio Piana, 1953.

_____. *Summa Theologiae*. 2nd rev. edition. Translated by Fathers of the English Dominican Province, 1920. Online edition by Kevin Knight, 2017, at Newadvent.org.

Britt, Matthew, O.S.B. *The Hymns of the Breviary and Missal*. New York: Benziger Brothers, 1936.

Chesterton, G. K. *St. Thomas Aquinas*. Reprint of 1943 edition. Brooklyn, Angelico Press, 2011.

Connelly, Joseph. *Hymns of the Roman Liturgy*. Westminster, MD: The Newman Press, 1957.

Eco, Umberto. *The Aesthetics of Thomas Aquinas*. Translated by Hugh Bredin. Cambridge: Harvard University Press, 1988.

Gilson, Etienne. *The Christian Philosophy of St. Thomas Aquinas*. Translated by L. K. Shook. New York: Random House, 1956.

Harmon, William, and C. Hugh Holman. *A Handbook to Literature*. 7th edition. Upper Saddle River, NJ: Prentice-Hall, 1996.

Pieper, Joseph. *Guide to Thomas Aquinas*. Translated by Richard and Clara Winston. New York: New American Library, 1964.

McInerny, Ralph. *St. Thomas Aquinas*. Notre Dame; University of Notre Dame Press, 1982.

Suñol, Dom Gregory. O.S.B. *Text Book of Gregorian Chant*. Tournai: Desclée and Socii, 1930.

Uitti, Karl D. *Linguistics and Literary Theory*. New York: Norton, 1969.

Weisheipl, James, O.P. *Friar Thomas Aquino.: His Life, Thought, and Work*. Garden City: Doubleday, 1964.